THE HARV

The mortals who merit God's boon
Could probably fill a platoon;
But the noblest on earth
Are the masters of mirth
Who write jokes for the Harvard Lampoon.

VARD LAM

POON BIG

This book is dedicated to Elmer Green, 1897-1977 Grand Curator of the Lampoon for forty-seven years.

BOOK OF

COLLEGE I

Edited by
Steven G. Crist
and
George Meyer

Staff Writers: Allan Arffa, Steven G. Crist, Ann Hodgman, Brian McCormick, George Meyer, David Owen, Roger Parloff, Mitchell Pross, Charles Stephen

Staff Artist: Mel J. Horan

Managing Editor: Steven G. Crist

A Dolphin Book
Doubleday & Company, Inc.
Garden City, New York
1978

LIFE

A Dolphin Book
Doubleday & Company, Inc.
ISBN: 0-385-13446-0
Library of Congress Catalog Card Number 77-15165
Copyright © 1978 by the Harvard Lampoon, Inc.
Printed in the United States of America
9 8 7 6 5 4 3 2

Acknowledgment and thanks are made for
permission to reprint—"Oh, Yes, You Should Go To
College" which originally appeared in *Oui* magazine,
copyright © 1976 by Playboy Publications, Inc.

ACKNOWLEDGMENTS

The Editors would like to thank the following individuals for the advice, assistance and money they contributed to this book:

Doug Ames, Tim Atkeson, George Beal, Jim Collins, The Harvey Cox Family, Downing, Peter Eastwood, Sam Fogler and the staff of Typo Tech, The Girlathoners, Lindy Hess, Rob Hoffman, Ken Kleppert, Ruth Liebmann, Malka, Kay Matschullat, Richard Pan, Melanie Pulik, Eric Rayman, Rooster Cogburn, J.C. Suarès, Sultry Sister and Susan Willmarth. Some of these names are those of racing greyhounds.

TABLE OF

CONTENTS

*Important
Message —*

see page 186

HARVARD LAMPOON

OUT TODAY

FOREWORD

The book you are now holding is the culmination of over sixty man-hours of nail-breaking effort. It tips the scales with ease, and boasts more than 11 color illustrations — all too big to fit on the period at the end of this sentence. If the pages were laid end to end they could circle a Cadillac *five times!* It is a tribute to modern publishing that this volume can be brought to you, the consumer, for only $1.95 (slightly higher in the U.S.). Of course, no work of this magnitude writes itself. Your copy is, rather, the end product of four integrated steps: *writing down, editing out, printing up* and *selling them*. Let's look at just one segment of the publishing process, the writing.

First, accommodations are secured. Before anything is ever committed to paper, a research staff begins an intensive study of the local media for the dates and locations of rock concerts, auto races, wet T-shirt contests, and other cultural events. These "sacred cows" will serve as ready targets for the book's roving satirical eye. Cooling beverages provide protection from the sun's blazing rays. The television is always left on for important news bulletins. Just before sunset each day, women begin beating on washtubs to frighten the tiny mammals into waiting nets. In this way, the manuscript is quickly completed.

Originally, the book was not to be sold in stores, but through a well-known manufacturer of bottle 'n' jug cutters, meal sealers, and tiny electric fishing rods. In the eleventh hour, Doubleday submitted the winning bid, $680,000, for paperback rights. However, we adamantly refused their mercenary proposal that some 50 pages be devoted to ads for sex toys, magnetic crosses, and flying saucer magazines. The line has to be drawn somewhere.

The writers of this anthology are a diverse group. The only common bond which ties us all together is a tremendous love for one thing: the films of Bing Crosby. When not writing, we each pursue a different avocation. For instance, Ann collects tortures people would like to use on Son of Sam. David collects "anything Xeroxed" and George likes to observe the sun with binoculars "so it doesn't try anything." Steve enjoys playing the home versions of *The Dating Game* and *Supermarket Sweep* when everyone else is asleep. Everyone else likes to sleep.

Disraeli once said that the quality which distinguishes man from the beasts is his ability to pay too much for a book. Shaw wryly added, "... and not ask for a refund." In all seriousness, though, we have but one objective in writing this book. If only one person buys it, and finds something inside to smile at or perhaps chuckle at, then we will lose many thousands of dollars and have to start selling handguns to schoolchildren .

The wacky crew of *S.S. Lampy* cries "Fun Ahoy!" on its maiden voyage through the sleazy seas of book publishing. Wishing the reader well are Gilligan (Steven Crist), The Skipper too (Brian McCormick), The Millionaire (George Meyer) and His Wife (Bill Johnsen), The Movie Star (Max Pross), The Professor (David Owen) and Mary Ann (Ann Hodgman).

Section

1

Before The Fall: Pre-college

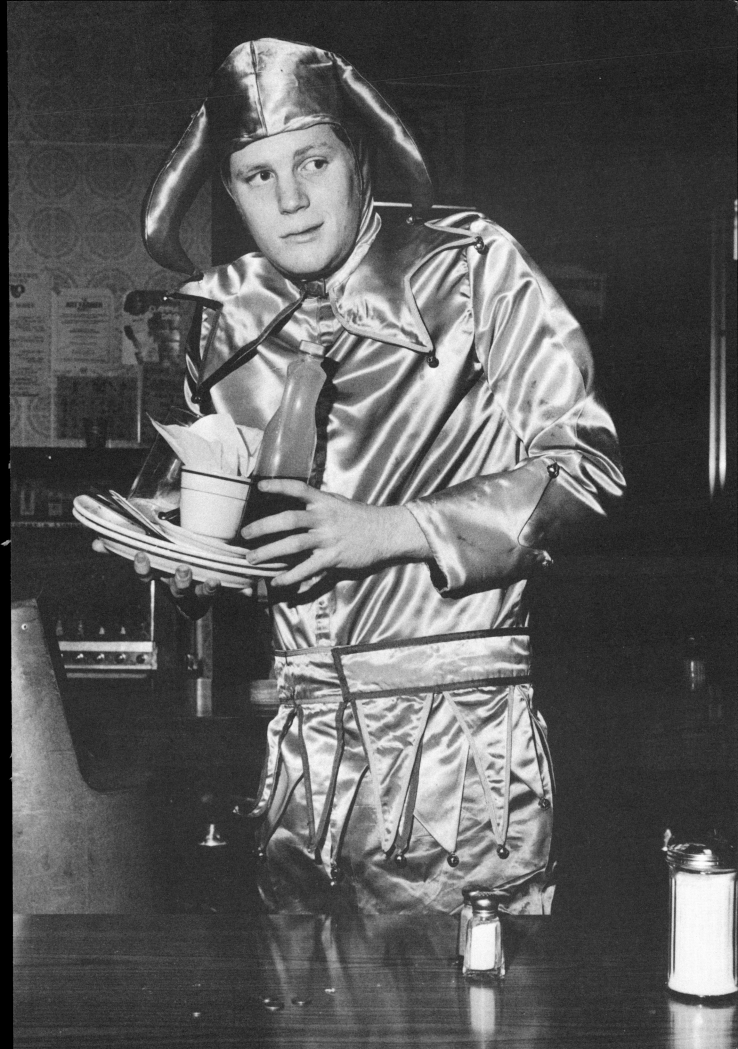

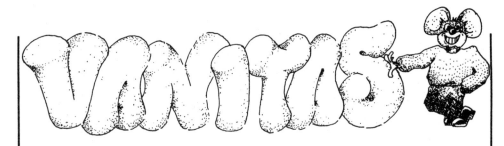

VANITAS

If you are a high school senior who has spent his Friday nights studying chemistry, blown cool autumn afternoons in a study carrel or watched wild dances from behind a student council refreshment stand, then you will undoubtedly plan to attend a good college. And why not? You are certainly entitled to it; having just wasted the "best years of your life," you must feel entitled to some compensation. A "good college," of course, is an institution where you can continue to believe that there is something to live for after graduation, study romantic novels that will never be made into movies, use calculators as if they were pinball machines and eat on well-balanced meal plans — all to the exclusion of anything humanly enjoyable.

As for high school's covering the "best years of your life," this is a misconception. Science has now proven that years 18 to 24 are the best, *the years you are in college.* In fact, the high school years are not even runner-up — that honor goes to years 50 to 54, with years 14 to 18 only receiving a special judges' prize awarded at an obscure festival in Switzerland. What this means is that good times wasted in college are times that can *never be enjoyed again*—unlike other times, for which reasonable facsimiles may turn up later. Right this second, if you are in college and are not dead drunk or with a girl or with a dead girl, you are letting precious time slip by — time so valuable that you are losing about five thousand dollars a day in monetary terms. You are well on your way to bankruptcy.

The point is obvious without being well taken. You don't want to go to a good college. High school students can no longer live this lie. Your conviction that there is a future to look forward to, your attitude of "Well, I've worked hard these past few years and have never taken a girl to a drive-in, but it will all be worth it once I get into a good college!" is completely farcical, a shameful sham. We don't like to name names or anything, but we go to what is generally considered a good school, and we've made a number of observations:

1. It's very hard. Someone was overheard just a second ago saying, "I feel like taking a girl to a popular drive-in movie tonight, but with all the time-consuming work I have, I simply cannot do so."

2. There are no girls around here. Remember the way all the girls in high school went out with college guys? Well, that was when you were in high school. Sociologists have discovered a recent trend: immediately after your graduation, high school girls start going out with high school boys. College girls, however, go out only with older men, men who are out in the business world making lots of money to foster that older look. Many went to bad colleges, and they wear those schools' rings and T-shirts to prove it. The girls go crazy.

3. There are no drive-ins. All of the movie theaters near this "good college" are small, expensive, and have lobbies that you could not drive into *even if you had a car at school.* The films shown are all in French, have no radioactive monsters, and

the violence is always implied, never bloody. The comedies contain the kind of universal themes that no one thinks is funny.

This should crush any notion that a "good college" is something to look forward to. However, many will claim that another four years is not much to sacrifice for the next fifty, which will be enjoyed in style and comfort once that "good" diploma is hanging up on the wall, covering up that ghastly crack. We admire the youthful optimism in this opinion, but laugh hysterically because it is stupid. Please allow the lying voices of experience to clarify a few things.

If you constantly chased grades in high school, you must remember how insufferable you were. You don't? Well, you were. We're sorry. We're all sorry. But let's face it, nobody could stand you. That girl you always liked, L8=$ie 2@3mt+berg, told us she thought you were particularly repellent. (That is a legitimate typographical error; it was not placed there purposely because we don't know her name.) The fact is that in high school you did not have to put up with yourself; others did. If you go to this "good school" you've been whining about, you'll find that everyone there is exactly like you. Don't be fooled by the "diverse student body" routine.

To begin with, everyone there is as smart and cunning as you, only worse because they were warned earlier and have been preparing. Mandatory remedial courses are assigned to students with sub-700 board scores, and the custodial crew is chosen from freshmen whose application essays "failed to entertain" the admissions office. Secondly, everyone knows not only the same amount, but the same things. Amazingly, each student took identical Advanced Placement courses in secondary school, read the same books and listened to the same music in an attempt to be "different." Simply because a school has geographical distribution quotas, don't think that the funny-looking student from Swaziland is any more interesting than you are. Go up to him and find out. "Grew up in Swaziland, hey fella? Bet you have quite a few experiences different from those found in my own culture that you could relate to me over a couple of exotic drinks!" Wrong. Not only has the boy been brought up on Stuckey's peanut brittle and reruns of *The Brady Bunch,* but his parents cautioned him about embarrassing cultural giveaways before sending him to America. He was instructed to act "Western," so he won't be using beer as shampoo or spearing cyclists. There goes any "foreign" enlightenment or entertainment you might have wanted.

There is, of course, the option of going to a bad school. Here you would have more intelligence than the other students. You would be "different." Although good grades would be easier to obtain, we all know what happens to people who are "different." You will be hated as you were in high school, branded as a mutant and exposed to painful shock therapies. You will be known as Double-Dome or Brainiac. So forget it.

The question that remains is whether a "good school" is still worth the time and money, in light of all that we have discussed. It reminds one of the classic story of the kangaroo in the bar who, when told of the rarity of his species in such an establishment, replies, "And at these prices, I'm not surprised." Except for the fact that we are students at a good university and students are not rare at universities, the analogy is apt. Also, a bar is a good place to be and a good college is a bad place to be. But the prices only make it worse. As far as sex and violence go you might as well skip college altogether and go directly into organized crime. Also, kangaroos have pouches and students don't.

"BUT ARE YOU SURE YOU CAN GET IN?"

High school guidance counselors serve two functions: (1) to get the college-bound students into college, and (2) to keep the non-college-bound students out of jail.

A high school is accredited every few years by a committee of gentlemen from the board of education who intimidate the teachers by sitting in on classes and giggling while jotting things down in little black books. When they are not roaming the halls in a mob "checking" the girls' rooms, these men examine the school's records. The most important factor in determining the rating the school receives is the number of college acceptances granted the school's students. If this number is low, the principal loses his job and the town gets a new bar.

This is why the principal puts pressure on the guidance counselors to concentrate more on function #1 and less on function #2; since a society does not need non-college-bound students, they might as well end up on jail. Guidance counselors are usually crusty middle-aged women who claim to have great rapport with people, but when asked why they never married tend first to clear their throats voluntarily and then gag involuntarily. If they value their jobs, friends and families, guidance counselors will always be glad to help a conscientious student get into college—any college.

STUDENT: Knock knock.

GUIDANCE COUNSELOR: You don't have to say "knock knock." Knocking on the door is enough.

STUDENT: Oh. Hello, Mrs. Buttle.

COUNSELOR: Hello, Steven.

STUDENT: Bernard. Bernard Weissman. I'm a senior here and I—

COUNSELOR: Please excuse me for not remembering your name. It's just that I don't know who you are. Where have you been, in prison?

STUDENT: I haven't been in prison. I met you at the beginning of ninth grade when you helped me plan my schedule. Since then I've been studying hard and racking up good grades. I came today for some help in choosing a college.

COUNSELOR: Oh, of course. You know, mmfhtujd jjjoeghj llkjqiie.

STUDENT: Oh, I know exactly what you mean.

COUNSELOR: No you don't. I was talking gibberish. I wanted to see how ingratiating you could be. Anyway, you're here to talk college. First of all, are you sure you want to go? I mean, four years is a long time, and there's good money to be made at Hamburger Choo Choo operating those little trains that bring the burgers to the customers. No college education necessary—

STUDENT: No, no. I'm sure I want to go. I've worked real hard for it.

COUNSELOR: Of course. But are you sure you can get in? You see, it doesn't look good for the school to have a lot of our applicants rejected. After all, not everyone can go to college.

STUDENT: I've done well in school, and have looked forward to college since I first realized that college grads make up most of the higher income bracket.

COUNSELOR: Splendid. What did you have in mind—one of the two-year junior colleges?

STUDENT: Frankly, Mrs. Buttle, I'd planned to apply to some of the better four-year schools.

COUNSELOR: Of course, of course, but remember—each application has to be okayed by the guidance department and the principal. I hope you don't plan on applying to *too* many of the state schools.

STUDENT: Er... actually, I wasn't going to apply to any state schools. I was kind of figuring on going east to a prestigious liberal arts school. My grades are pretty good. You can look at my transcript. It's right in front of you.

COUNSELOR: Oh yes. Hmmm. Well, there's a rumor going around that you should apply to as many schools as you can—after all, what's a 15-dollar application fee where your whole life is concerned? This isn't the time to be lazy—you may get lucky and get into a really good school.

Well, Benny, this is a very foolish attitude. I tell all my students *not* to waste their time filling out long application forms. Apply only where you're positive you can get in. Not only does a rejection make this high school look bad, but why endure all the personal heartbreak and humiliation when you can get it from me? Besides, 15 dollars is a lot of money, money you'll need for tuition and bribes at *your* college next year. Also, colleges don't like it when you apply to lots of schools. Each school likes to feel that it's your first choice. Naturally, the colleges have no way of knowing that you fed the same butt-sucking essay to fifty different schools. However, if someone on the admissions committee should ask me to recommend you, I might have to tell him the painful truth. It's not that I don't like you, it's just that it hurts me to lie.

STUDENT: I'm not asking you to lie. I thought I'd apply to a few of the top schools, and then a safety. I was hoping you could suggest which ones might be best suited for—

COUNSELOR: I can tell you right now. The one and only school you need apply to is Finster.

STUDENT: Finster? I don't think I've ever heard of it.

COUNSELOR: Finster Barber College. Best school of its kind in the country. Maybe Canada, too.

STUDENT: What? Barber College?

COUNSELOR: Well, your grades are pretty good. There's no reason why you shouldn't reach the top of the lot.

STUDENT: Mrs. Buttle, I have an A-plus average and I took all Advanced Placement courses. I have a 1590 combined SAT score. I'm class valedictorian, president of the student council and manager of the football team. I can't play because of my glasses, and the doctor won't let me have contacts. To tell you the truth, I was hoping to go to Harvard, Princeton or Yale.

COUNSELOR: Those are good schools, but fairly limited in the barber sciences...

STUDENT: But I don't want to be a barber! I want to be a doctor.

COUNSELOR: Well, I suppose you could apply to medical schools after a few years at Finster. What kind of extracurricular activities have you participated in that involve haircuts?

STUDENT: Uh, none. But I don't *want* to go to a barber school.

COUNSELOR: Oh, I get it, you think you can just open a shop just like that, with no training? You want to start snipping away right after high school?

STUDENT: Look, couldn't I just apply to the Ivies? I'm pretty sure I can get into one of them. I want to major in chemistry.

COUNSELOR: Let me be blunt. According to a Vocational Aptitude Test given to you in the guise of an English Achievement Exam, the occupations most compatible with your talents are barber and hood ornament. And since you're obviously not a chrome-plated eagle, I can only assume that the barberhood is where you're headed.

STUDENT: But surely those tests don't mean anything.

COUNSELOR: Only to the colleges that receive your transcript.

STUDENT: This is ridiculous. I'm sending applications to Harvard and Yale. They'll disregard the VAT when they see my grades and find out that I went to biology camp.

COUNSELOR: Well, all I can say is that I'll hope for the best and "approve" your applications, but I know I really won't. I'm not saying chemistry and calculus aren't important, but you should be able to shape and not just trim. Kids today want it kept long, but thinned out a little.

*   *   *   *   *

Bernard Weissman ignored his experienced guidance counselor's advice. He was rejected by all of the five Ivy League schools he applied to. He now works at Hamburger Jungle, cleaning up after the wild animals that serve burgers to the customers.

Joe Morono, a "hood" who used to "scare" Bernard in high school, wisely followed his guidance counselor's advice and applied to Finster as his first and only choice. He was accepted, graduated with honors, and went to work for Sam of Sam's Barbershop fame. Within three years he opened his own chain of Unisex shops in Manhattan and Hollywood. For fun, he styles hair for Farrah and Bianca. Annual Income: $350,000.

HARVARD · RADCLIFFE

Committee on Admissions
Byerly Hall, 8 Garden Street
Cambridge, Massachusetts 02138

April 14, 1978

Ms. Brenda Handl
124 Glenroad Rd.
Rochester, NY 14604

Dear Ms. Handl:

I am sorry to inform you that you did not receive any form of acceptance at Harvard-Radcliffe. While I am, indeed, sorry, as stated above, I am also glad in a way, for you will now be able to consider a wide variety of opportunities, ones which it is very possible you have not considered until this exact instant. In that way, you should perhaps think of this letter as a "passport" to a new--as yet unchartered--way of life, or sea voyage.

It is not easy for me to have to write this kind of letter, and I know it must make you very sad, but it is my job. I am not mean by nature, and I do not wish you to think harshly of me, so I will give you a little illustration to make my point. Once there was a young woman (not you) who wished to attend an excellent university, but what she really wanted to do was to get married and spend all her time entering flower shows. But her grades were very good, but she took herself too seriously, and didn't shave her legs, so she was almost admitted, but then at the last minute she wasn't. Whiff this, "Ms." so-called Handl: it was you! No, just kidding, no offense. It was in fact someone else, and in any case she was admitted.

I hope that my anecdote will increase your sense of penis envy --whoops! I mean, self-assurance. You should not feel that this decision in any way reflects on you as a person, or on your abilities or unpleasant skin condition. As you are undoubtedly aware, many zillions of thoroughly qualified applicants are turned away each year simply because they are not admitted to Harvard-Radcliffe. Some of these applicants are famous, too, while others, embittered by their rejection letters, become cheapened and turn to lives of crime and deception. Which are you? Only time will tell, but time heals all wounds: sculpt it into any bandage you choose.

Finally, I would like to suggest that you bracket the above **para**graph and leave this letter for your mother to find. I greatly enjoyed our little chat when she called the Admissions Office a week or so ago. Good-bye.

Sincerely,

Bob ☺

Robert "The Man" Avery
Director of Admissions

R"M"A:edc
no enclosures

Mr. Elmer Green

180 Riverside Drive

New York, New York

10024

PRINGLE COLLEGE

TERRE HAUTE, INDIANA

LET PRINGLE CHOOSE YOU

"The man doesn't choose the college, the college chooses him."

Rousseau said something to that effect more than a century ago; it's still true today. More young people than ever are exploring compatible lifestyles in a liberal arts environment. Some are drawn to highly competitive, emotionally sterilizing Ivy League schools; others are attracted to the impersonality and isolation of enormous state universities or the nosiness and intolerance of small rural colleges. And every year some seven hundred students find themselves under the spell of Pringle College, a school different from, and yet somehow better than, every other institution of higher learning.

Founded in 1921, Pringle was chartered as "a coeducational undergraduate college licensed to grant the degree of Bachelor of Arts" (Ind. Res. 106783). This spirit still pervades the Pringle campus today. Down through the years the college has graduated many notable figures who have expressed the Pringle Idea in their own ways: Hank Anderson, Rosemary Casals, Margaret Truman Daniel, Virgil Fox, Vance Hartke, Barbara Howar, Jack Jones, William Lundigan, Dr. William Masters, Nicholas Ray, Carl Sagan, Max Schulman. Most of these old Pringlers attend the annual reunions, held yearly.

But I guess we know well enough that history doesn't interest the college-bound. Today's young people make their stand on the bottom line. And when it comes to the bottom line, we think that Pringle speaks for itself. So give this leaflet a cursory glance, and the next time you're in the drugstore just amble over to the paperback rack and pick up a Pringle application. You'll be glad you did.

I can't close my remarks with anything more fitting than this line from our own Dean Bostwick: "Academics **is**, and Pringle **is** academics." Aloha.

Harold Lemoyne
President, Pringle College

Pringlers learn the
new 3 R's—record,
repeat and relate—in
the language lab.

THE BUCK TALKS HERE.

President Harold
Lemoyne spearheads
Pringle's ongoing
fund drive.

"This England!"

— William Shakespeare

That's the feeling that overwhelms most pilgrims to the campus of Pringle College, lovely as the "scepter dial" of the Bard's immortal song. Nestled in the rolling flatland of central Indiana, the school grounds comprise more than three square miles, including a model farm.

After a leisurely drive out from Terre Haute (not forgetting to stop for film and cornburgers at one of the roadside stands that dot the countryside) you, the prospective student, will soon find yourself at the first Pringle landmark — our gaily colored admission booth. We suggest that you make a seventy-five cent donation to the Pringle Scholarship Fund, a division of the Student Lounge and Activities Council.

Park your car (no tipping!) and then stroll along a carpet of Astrolite to Benjamin Harrison Hall, the cornerstone that spurs the pulse of Pringle. Once a historic corrections facility, Harrison Hall is now consecrated to our twenty-third President and the administrative tasks he performed so unflinchingly. It is in Harrison that the great events of college life occur: registration, the posting of grades and the notification of assignment to fraternities and sororities.

Before looking in on the dormitories and recreational facilities, you may wish to inspect the classrooms, laboratories and libraries (that's right — we have all three) in which students are expected to spend several hours a day. These rooms are reserved for visitors only from 9 to 11 a.m., 2 to 10 p.m. and all day Friday, Saturday and Sunday. We bet you won't be able to resist the urge to plunk yourself down in a seat and experience firsthand the suspense of finding out whether or not a lecture will be held. After that dose of academic rigor, you'll want to tour the Pringle Museum, complete with authentic 1890s Ferris wheel and shooting gallery (don't forget your complimentary pony ride in the zoological annex!).

But all work and no play makes Jack a dull boy. Every visitor loves to drop in at the undergraduate lounge and enjoy a first-run movie or a prize match between prospective athletic scholarship recipients. Good-natured Pringlers are always available for a "pick-up" game of volleyball (coed, of course!) and afterward a friendly and informative chat in the double occupancy locker rooms of the clubhouse.

Tired at the end of a typical Pringle day, you'll be pleased to discover your "dorm" is only footsteps away — and not even that, when you ride our Buckminster Fuller soon-to-be Memorial People Mover. Let your aching dogs play dead while the moving sidewalk escorts you to your air-conditioned room. Once you've settled in, you may experience a little of the loneliness of the first night at college. Don't be afraid to reach out — somebody may well be there. And, naturally, don't forget to bring a supply of quarters.

Next morning, edified and refreshed, you'll down a hearty breakfast of chemically enriched orange or tomato juice that will see you chipper through the day. Just a hop, skip and a stagger from the dining hall door your car will be waiting, as polished and shining as the smiles of our garage attendants. (Remember — no tipping!). As you tool down our meandering drive, thinking back on what you've observed during your stay at Pringle College, you'll realize that, for our students, the long hours of loafing, gambling, drinking and making out are all worthwhile.

FACULTY AND CURRICULUM

Classes at Pringle involve more than the memorization of dry facts to be spewed out again on unimaginative exams; they provide a valuable framework for the the time between sauna and luncheon. Ever since 1921 (excepting the war years) classes have filled this central role admirably, and the annual faculty vote for their continuance is almost taken for granted.

What's taught in Pringle courses? You name it. Under the "Departmental System" (instituted in 1949) each area of human knowledge, such as Trees, The Roaring Twenties or Actors and Their Roles, has its own department and faculty. Once selected for a particular faculty, a professor may spend months learning about his subject. As Dean of the Faculty Bostwick put it, "The Departmental System puts the 'expert' in 'experience.'"

He might have added, "and a good thing for students, too." He certainly would have been right. Whether it's Hibachi Cookery, Personal Banking or Ecodumping, students are the main beneficiaries of classes taught by informed teachers.

That's why we encourage every Pringler to take courses. Imagine discussing a Dylan lyric with Pulitzer Prize-winning poetess Phyllis McGinley; building your own home entertainment center with tips from internationally ranked physicists; learning about makeup from a real circus clown. And through all the fun, looking forward to that later reward — a heaping plate of quiche Lorraine.

FEES AND APPLICATIONS

Many students needlessly worry about the commitment and expense of four or six years at college. Try to put the problem in perspective. Ask yourself these questions:

1. Did God give me intelligence, independence, curiosity, wealthy parents, perseverance? Does He want me to make use of them?
2. Do my parents want me to be happy? Would they pay for an abortion or marital annulment to make me happy?
3. Do I like people my own age doing things I'd like to do? Would I like to be like them?
4. Do I want to be a good person? To fall in love?
5. Will I get a new car for graduation this spring?

There are no easy answers to these questions. But if you find your own reply is "Yes" to all of them (or at least 1, 2 and 5), Pringle has chosen you. Send in an application to this address:

Busitronic Confidata
Vesco Park
Bird in Hand, PA 17505

In order not to embarrass scholarship students unduly, we require **all** applicants to include a copy of their parents' most recent tax return. If time is short, the tax statement will be accepted in lieu of application. Allow ten days for processing and mailing of acceptance and specific information on fees.

PANEM·ET·CIRCENSES

PRINGLE·MCMXC

**PRINGLE—THE
PROUD NEW
WRINKLE
IN EDUCATION**

Applicant's Full Name: (Print) Backslap Mike Bob Jr. Date of Birth Oct. 6 / 1950
Last   First   Middle   Jr., etc.   month day   year

It will help us greatly if you will file your application within *two weeks* after you receive it.

Application for Admission to Harvard College in 1968

A. ACTIVITIES

-winner of NEDT award/participant in National Educational Development Test

In answering the following questions (and throughout this form) please mention nothing which would indicate your race, creed, color or national origin. (This is in accordance with Massachusetts law.)

-selected by College Entrance Examination Board for participation in Scholastic Aptitude

List any scholastic distinctions or honors you have won since the ninth grade. ↳Testing program

-winner of recognition citation from National Educational Development Testing Service

-participant in Scholastic Aptitude Test tutoring program/winner of NEDT award

-cited for outstanding performance on NEDT exam/Perfect Attendance medal/Spanish Club

Please list your principal extracurricular and community activities (excluding jobs) during *term-time* in your secondary school years *in the order of their interest for you.* (for example: student government, athletics, debating, church group, 4-H Club, Boy Scouts, dramatics, publications, hobbies.)

Activity	Approximate dates of participation	Approximate number of hours spent per week	Positions held or honors won
Student Council President/chairman of SGA Ad Hoc Committee on the Powers of SGA President			
Voting member of Student Government Association/winner of Student Council presidential			
Freshman football team/SGA President/Student Council Dance Committee/ Selection			
Sophomore football team/Student Government President/nominated for Student Council Pres.			
Student Council Executive Board (Chairman)/Speaker at Student Council Convention			
Led ticket in Student Council Presidential Election/Chairman of SGA steering committee			
Varsity football (junior year)/Chief Executive Officer of Student Government Association			
Varsity football (senior year)/President of Student Council/Spanish Club			
ALSO: selected for participation in CEEB Achievement Test program/Good Posture award			

B. WORK EXPERIENCE

Please list any jobs (including summer employment) you may have held in the past three years.

Job	Employer	Approximate dates of employment	Approximate no. of hours spent per wk.	Approximate total amount earned
operator of Student Council mimeograph machine				volunteer work
~~baby-sat for brother-in-law~~/organized volunteer child	care center			volunteer work
Spanish Club				

C. List the books you have read during the past twelve months. Place an "x" after those required in school courses. Summer reading suggested by a department at school should be listed without an "x". (A separate sheet with your name on it may be used if necessary.) List at the end the magazines and newspapers you read regularly.

Recently my reading has grown in depth rather than breadth. It has been chiefly concerned with the problems and promise of higher education in America:

Barron's Profile of American Colleges/Scoring High on College Entrance Examinations
The Ivy League Guidebook/Barron's How to Prepare for the PSAT-NMSQT
Einstein's College Entrance Guide/Practice for Effective Writing
The Handbook of College Entrance Examinations/How to Prepare Your College Application
Six Weeks to Words of Power/Insider's Guide to the Colleges/Windsong
Barron's In-Depth Guide to the Ivy League Schools/Practice for Scholastic Aptitude Tests
Push Comes to Shove: The Escalation of Student Protest at Harvard/Rapid Vocabulary Builde
New York Times 1968 Guide to College Selection/Six Minutes a Day to Perfect Spelling
Arco Test Tutor-National Merit Scholarship Tests/The New American Guide to Colleges
How to be Accepted at the College of Your Choice/30 Days to a More Powerful Vocabulary
Arco Test Tutor-Scholastic Aptitude Test/Correctness and Effectiveness of Expression
Harvard Through Change and Storm/Lovejoy's College Guide/Writing a Good Essay

On this page write (or type, if convenient) the essay requested in question I. on page 4 of this application.

What does Harvard mean? It means many things to many people. I guess to me it's a myriad of images and associations. It's Widener Library at twilight. It's watching the crew races from Weeks Bridge. It's George Wald's Origin of Death lecture. It's Vic Gatto crossing the Eli five-yard line to bring victory to the Cantabs. It's Eliot House. It's John Finley.

What do I want out of Harvard? It's really hard to say. I guess I just want to live life to the fullest by sampling the various channels of experience which lie open to the intellectually curious. But it's more than that. I want to find out who this funny little guy called Mike Backslap really is. I am a very deep person, continually moving, expanding, growing, changing, probing into new areas of experience. I myself would not have it any other way. For education is a drawing out, not a pumping in. And the man who graduates today and stops learning tomorrow is uneducated the day after. War is not healthy for children and other living things. And I sincerely feel that if I were admitted to Harvard, there would be no more wars.

In all honesty, I guess there is one personal problem of mine I should discuss in this essay. I've never been able to do anything just halfway. I don't take up a project; I embrace it. I crush it to my bosom. All the way. 100%. No turning back. My friends tell me I'm a fool. But I don't care. It's all or nothing for me. And I, for one, would not have it differently.

I don't want any answers out of Harvard. I just want to learn how to ask the right questions. Harvard can do a hell of a lot for me. And I can do a lot for Harvard.

Applicant's Full Name:	Backslap	Mike	Bob	Jr.	Date of	10 / 6 / 1950
(Please print)	Last	First	Middle	Jr., etc.		Month Day Year

Please return this questionnaire within one week after its receipt if possible.

HARVARD COLLEGE

Teacher's Report on Applicant

Please tell us what you can about his intellectual qualities and his academic work. We are interested in any evidence you can give us about the nature of his motivation for academic work, the breadth and depth of his intellectual interests, the originality, independence, sensitivity and power of his mind, and his capacity for growth. Is he, for instance, excessively grade-conscious or driven by family pressure? Does he have to be nursed or prodded, or is he genuinely interested? What are your impressions of his character, aims and values? Does he have any unusual competence, talent, or capacity for leadership?

Although I have known Mike only a short time, I have heard on many occasions of the nature of his motivation for academic work, the breadth and depth of his intellectual interests, the originality, independence, sensitivity and power of his mind, and his capacity for growth. He is, in addition, excessively grade conscious and driven by family pressure, factors which should insure that the level of his academic output remains high. I have often known Mike to be nursed and prodded. I also know, for example, that he is a member of the Spanish Club.

Overall, I feel that Mike's unusual competence, talents, and capacity for leadership, coupled with my impressions of his character, aims and values, mark him as a top candidate for your school. I am sure that, should you accept him, Mike will prove to be for you a source of pleasure and intellectual content both now in these our troubled times and in the years that lie ahead.

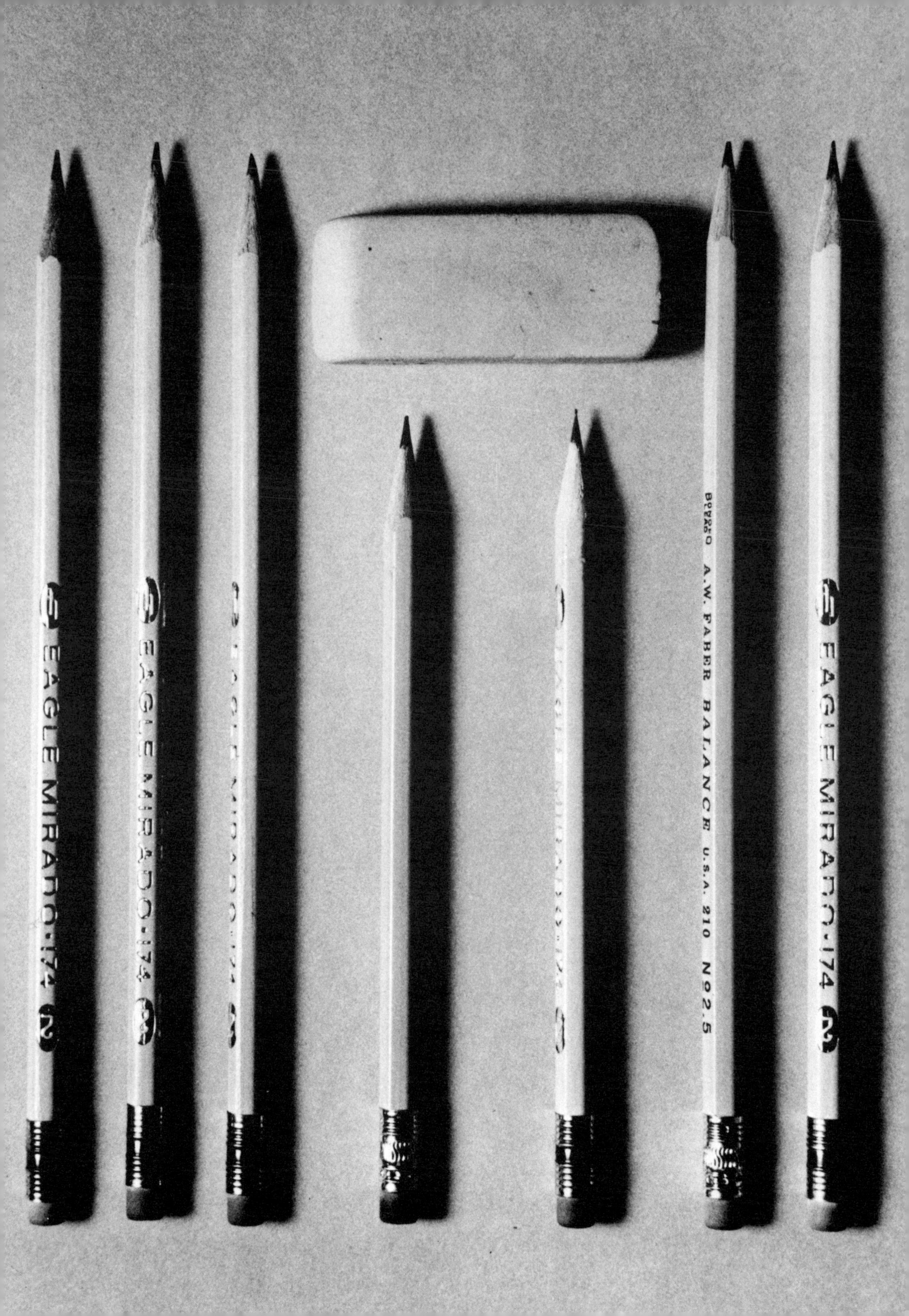
EAGLE MIRADO·174
EAGLE MIRADO·174
A.W. FABER BALANCE U.S.A. 210 №2.5
EAGLE MIRADO·174

1978
UNNECESSARY STUDENT APTITUDE TEST (UNSAT)

TEST TO BE ADMINISTERED ON:
Thursday, September 4
OR
Wednesday, September 10

DO NOT OPEN THIS BOOK UNTIL EVERYONE ELSE DOES.

GENERAL DIRECTIONS

Read these directions while the supervisor needlessly reads them out loud. You will be given two hours to work this test. The supervisor will tell you when it is time to begin. Remember that it is unimportant how you "do" on any test. What matters is that you and your assessors know how well you understand the material. Sure.

This is a test designed to appraise your appropriateness as a college student. You will be judged on your credibility, suitability, geekability and general acumen. As a junior humanoid, you will be able to judge from your test results whether you should apply to college or drop out and get a low-paying job.

Part A—Analogies

DIRECTIONS: Choose from the five pairs one pair that seems most likely to you to have the same relationship of its first part to its second part as the one that we call the "question." Then indicate it to the computer.

EXAMPLE:
BOONDOGGLE : BUNWARMER:
(A). poontang : suntan
(B). dormitory : dromedary
(C). boonwarmer : bundoggle
(D). lavatory: lovebead
(E). godsend : ginseng

Letter "D" is obviously correct. This is, of course, a simple example; the real questions require some knowledge of Latin verb roots.

1. PORKY : PINE
    (A) forky : fine
    (B) fat : tree
    (C) cat : pee
    (D) armor : dildo
    (E) dorky : guy

2. CRAMP : STYLE
    (A) roommate : sex life
    (B) backseat : sex life
    (C) eat : candy
    (D) pamcr : yestl
    (E) menstrual : high

3. UNICEF CARDS : ART
    (A) starvation : Pieta
    (B) decal : diorama
    (C) Dondi : Dante
    (D) *Jaws : Leviathan*
    (E) hotcomb : when men were men

4. KNOWLEDGE : STUDENT
    (A) homo : hardhat
    (B) kryptonite: Superman
    (C) keys : kitten
    (D) bauxite : carnivores
    (E) shampoo : Maynard

5. SENIOR : FRESHMAN
    (A) Rogue elephant : village
    (B) tractors : topsoil
    (C) cocaine: rocksalt
    (D) Mothra: Osaka
    (E) acid : face

6. TICK : CANT
    (A) venus : regina
    (B) plick : clack
    (C) clock : pushy
    (D) torque : whole
    (E) harden : scratch

7. Draw the adorable fawn in the space provided below.

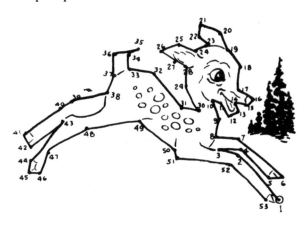

Part B—Sentence Completion

DIRECTIONS: If you have a minute, complete the sentences below by "plugging in" the choices until you find the "best" one.

8. Mr. Anderson has six toes and as a result can _____ with his _____.
    (A) argue .. wife
    (B) hobble along .. keeper
    (C) sing .. voice
    (D) defecate .. pants on
    (E) knit .. feet

9. When Arnie puts on his yodelling costume, there is no
   _____ for _____ .
   (A) time .. sergeants
   (B) bread .. poor people
   (C) outing .. instance
   (D) sonar .. the U-boat
   (E) way out .. any of you

10. Many people in our society have _____ , but it is not
    proper for others to make _____ of them because of it.
    (A) cancer .. slaves
    (B) hair .. wigs
    (C) brains .. mincemeat
    (D) rudders .. sailboats
    (E) vaginas .. women

11. The lead cheerleader at the state university _____
    every _____ of the football team.
    (A) blew .. chance
    (B) serviced .. school bus
    (C) pumped .. game ball
    (D) went down for .. game
    (E) petted .. mascot

12. When Professor Skinner was awakened by a funny
    _____ , he rushed to the telephone and called _____ .
    (A) smell .. for world peace
    (B) thought .. his students
    (C) martian .. the police
    (D) sleeping pill .. the hogs
    (E) tornado .. it a day

13. When Einstein checked his _____ , a peculiarity led
    him to believe that the universe was _____
    (A) lunch box .. hungry
    (B) books .. still there
    (C) horoscope .. unlucky
    (D) blood pressure .. unimportant
    (E) watch .. late

14. The food stamp program was initiated in the hopes
    that it would relieve the poor of some of the burden of
    nourishing themselves and their dependents. Many
    college students use the stamps to purchase _____ for
    their _____ .
    (A) tenderloin .. hamsters
    (B) ashtrays .. convenience
    (C) CB's .. bicycles
    (D) poor people .. amusement
    (E) helium .. lesbians

15. When a bird watcher takes his _____ into the forest,
    the first thing he looks for are _____ .
    (A) bazooka .. eagles
    (B) wife .. buzzards
    (C) woodpecker .. binoculars
    (D) television .. outlets
    (E) troubles .. psychiatrists

STOP!

**If you finish before time is up, go over your work
for this section only. Do not turn to any other
section of the test.**

Part A—Word Problems

DIRECTIONS: So you thought we finally wised up and decided to cut the Math Ability section altogether. Well, you were wrong about that.

1. If Brian is deprived of oxygen for an extended period of time, he will gradually lose consciousness and die. Inasmuch as he wishes to continue living, his parents have furnished his vacuum chamber with a 10-gallon container of water, a standard 12-volt automobile battery, and several yards of insulated wire. How long can Brian expect to live?
    (A) A few weeks.
    (B) Not long enough to make it worth his trouble to get a date for the high school prom.
    (C) Longer than some uncomplicated insects.
    (D) 100 years.
    (E) He may live, or he may not, but no one can drive an automobile without a battery.

2. Mathematics will be of use in later life because
    (A) the planet Earth is a geometric shape.
    (B) numbers are easier to write than words.
    (C) women cannot balance their checkbooks.
    (D) we "count on" our friends we do not "write on" them.
    (E) we will be replaced by machines.

3. Sandy has been invited to a formal banquet in another town. The town is 43 miles distant, and the wind is blowing at a steady 15 miles per hour from the west-northwest. Under ideal conditions, Sandy can expect to average 24 miles per hour on the road, which runs north to south. His automobile is in good condition and his driver is familiar with the route. A long embarrassing dent on the passenger side of the vehicle affects its wind resistance, but not significantly. The only real factor will be the crosswind. It is now 3:45. If Sandy leaves immediately, should he wear a white dinner jacket or a traditional black tuxedo?
    (A) The former.
    (B) The latter.
    (C) Either.
    (D) Forty-three miles is too far to travel for a formal "banquet."
    (E) There is no such thing as a "traditional" tuxedo.

Part B—Famous Writers School of Mathematics

DIRECTIONS: Each passage is excerpted from the work of a major literary artist. Read each passage, and answer the question it "asks." These are the only directions you are likely to get.

4. *Robert Frost*
    Whose woods these are I think I know.
    His house is ten miles distant though;
    He cannot see me stopping here
    En route from City "N" to "O."

    My little horse must think it queer
    (Our destination's hardly near)
    To stop mid woods and frozen lake
    As if the path ahead were clear.

    He gives his harness bells a shake
    To say, "Two hours more twill take!"
    The only other sound's the sweep
    Of easy wind, five m.p.h.

    The woods are lovely dark and deep.
    But I've a schedule to keep —
    How many miles before I sleep?
    Compute the miles before I sleep.
    (A) 5 miles
    (B) 500 miles
    (C) 10 farthings
    (D) 20,000 leagues
    (E) 1,280 feet

5. *Ernest Hemingway*
    The kitchen door opened and Nick and George came in. They sat down at the table. Nick lit a cigarette. So did George.
    "I have to mow the lawn," Nick said.
    "Oh," George said.
    "I figure it'll take two hours."
    "Oh."
    "How long would it take you?"
    George smoked. "An hour, maybe," he said.
    "How long would it take us together?"
    George looked out the window at the lawn. It looked green.
    (A) It would take Nick and George 3 hours.
    (B) It would take 2 chapters.
    (C) It would take half an hour.
    (D) At this rate, the lawn will never be mowed.
    (E) It would take "a twinkling of an eye."

6. *J. D. Salinger*
    If you really want to know about it, there used to be this guy named Gookfooser who had a lousy candy store way the hell down the street with a big sign in front that said "Gookfooser's Fine Confectionaries." *Fine Confectionaries.* That name killed me. It really did. The crap he sold was about as fine as a goddam toilet seat. Anyway, this Gookfooser was the most disgusting bastard I ever saw. He really was. He was always chewing on a goddam candy wrapper and clacking his lips like crazy. And then he had this dandruff that he was always *picking* at. He damn near made me vomit when he'd stick his dandruffy hands and all in a jar of nuts. He really did. And the windows of his store were always all smeared up, like some dog had just been *panting* on them. He didn't even *clean* them. I swear to God he didn't.
    Anyway, I used to go into that sunuvabitch's store to buy pecans. I *liked* them, if you want to know the

truth. I liked cashews better, but old Gookfooser charged 65 cents a pound for the pecans, and he had the cashews way the hell up at 80 cents. Eighty cents for cashews. That really killed me. Anyway, one day I went in and there was old Gookfooser, sucking on his goddam wrapper and clacking away for his life and scooping his goddam hands into the jars. Then he took some goddam pecans and cashews and started chucking them in a jar that said "Mixed Nuts." *Mixed Nuts.* That killed me. You could tell that Gookfooser was getting a big charge out of it, though, because he started clacking louder and spitting all over the place. I swear to God he did. You could see he thought I'd stand there and *ask* him what the hell he was charging for the nuts and all, the way he was clacking his goddam head off. People always expect you to ask them things. It bothers me. It really does. And so does the price of those goddam Mixed Nuts. I just can't figure it out. Maybe somebody else can, but I can't.

(A) I can. The answer is 75 cents.
(B) Uh-uh, pal, it's 80 cents.
(C.) Nope, a dollar.
(D) For your information, the answer is 85 goddam cents.
(E) Screw you, it's 90 cents.

STOP!

If you finish before time is up, go over your work for this section only. Do not turn to any other section of the test.

DIRECTIONS: This test is designed to "test" your abilities in the related areas of cooking, foodstuff skills, stove know-how and caloric values. You will be given a wide variety of questions in the text, so do not count on finding an easy section geared to your abilities. If you do not know an answer, *do not guess;* leave the question for another day. Inaccurate answers may lower your score and waste or ruin what would otherwise have been a perfectly good dish. Do not take this test on a damp day.

To help you in computing the answers, the following information has been provided:

1 bushel flour = 1 bushel acorn
  powder = 1 bushel fattening starch
  100 grams sugar = 100 cups sugar less 1 tablespoon
  16 apples minus 5 oranges = 3 apples
  1 gill fresh milk = 20 cups fresh Beluga caviar
  (Note: unsuccessful above sea level)
  1 ounce butter = 3 pounds butter
  1 cup raw chalk = 16 tablespoons grated white things
  (9,000 calories)

Begin the test. *Use correct answers.*

For each of the questions in this section you will be asked to choose the most appropriate response. Choose it.

1. What's that got to do with the price of _____ ?
   (A) eggs
   (B) coffee
   (C) beans
   (D) dogs
   (E) admission

2. Food cooked on an electric range has more "modern" taste than food cooked in a gasoline oven, but electric cooking adds calories to prepared foods. Depending on your financial clout, which is preferable, an electric range or a gas-powered range?
   (A) "I guess I'd rather have gas, because burner heat may more effectively be regulated on a stove with gas power."
   (B) "Definitely gas—I like the blue flame, and electric things are so *expensive.*"
   (C) "I think I'd choose an electric one, since that's the kind I own."
   (D) "I cook on hot stones. And you'd impress me a lot more if you'd put some pants on while you were talking to me."
   (E) "Well, the house is already set up for electricity. You can't argue with progress!"

3. Linda is alone in the house when a burglar enters and threatens to steal the jewels. To pacify him and stall for time, she offers to prepare him a "home- cooked meal with all the fixin's." Four hours later, she serves him fried chicken, biscuits, corn on the cob, crisp garden

salad and chocolate cream scrapes. Why did he kill her?

(A) On this diet, he'd *gain* weight, not lose it as he was hoping.
(B) While such a menu is well balanced and provides a variety in texture and color, it is perhaps rather heavy for such a hot, humid evening.
(C) The dinner is delicious, but the salad could have cooked a few minutes more.
(D) She sent him to the supermarket once too often.
(E) Any of the answers could be correct since the question provides only incomplete information.

STOP!

If you finish before time is up, go over your work for this section only. Do not turn to any other section of the test.

"I'm tired of working for that slavedriving boss!"
"I wish some crazy guy would shoot me!"

Ever talk like these fellows? Then maybe *you* have "what it takes" to become a senseless fatality. It isn't easy to become one of the "men who die by night"; statistics show that only 205 people were slain by hidden gunmen last year. Millions of guys like you want to be famous, hobnob with rich doctors, and leave a lot of money to their families, but . . . *they don't know how.* We can show you how. But first try this handy quiz.

DIRECTIONS: Answer the questions, buddy.

1. I am _____ .
    (A) an unremarkable loser with no relatives
    (B) a devoted dad of six, or a promising young nursing student who always has a ready smile

2. The buildings surrounding me are topped by _____ .
    (A) air-conditioning men
    (B) loners who were always excellent students

3. When I go out, it is just to _____ .
    (A) invite death by taunting psychopaths
    (B) buy a newspaper at the corner market.

4. When I am shot at, _____ .
    (A) the bullets miss me and break a lot of flowerpots
    (B) I lie down and blood pours out of me

5. I like to walk _____ .
    (A) on the surface of the moon or on the ocean floor
    (B) past grassy knolls, around shopping malls, on the sidewalk

6. My most recent picture _____ .
    (A) was taken yesterday, on a polo pony, by Richard Avedon
    (B) is in a blurry 1962 photo where I look best alongside twenty-six others

7. When I get up in the morning, the day starts out as _____ .
    (A) an ominous date with doom
    (B) just another ordinary day, like hundreds before it

8. My fondest dream is to _____ .
    (A) have my way with Princess Caroline in a sandbox full of cocaine
    (B) have the pavement around my dead body outlined with chalk

Were all your choices B? Great! For complete home-study information, write now. Don't wait until midnight tonight, or someone else might get the bullet with your name on it. Hurry.

—————◆●◆—————

Bunyan High SIXTY-THIRD ANNUAL HONORS ASSEMBLY
Bunyan High School
St. Paul, Minnesota

—————◆●◆—————

BRINGING IN OF THE FLAG .... Color Guard
PRAYER .... Pastor Pullman
BRIEF PRAYER .... Rabbi Schulman
WELCOME TO THIS ASSEMBLY .... Principal Wilson

MONSANTO YOUNG SCIENTIST SEARCH:
Grand Prize Winner:
"A Safe Cure for Heart Disease" .... Albert Darrow
Prize Winner:
"Orthomolecular Striation in Girls" .... Arthur Lubich
Honorable Mention:
"Farming the Skies" .... Allen Mitchell
Mention:
"Steam-Powered Fossil Finder" .... Arnold Castle
Awardee:
"Bouncing Radio Waves off People's Faces .... Alice Morse
Entrant:
"Rock Music Is Bad for House Plants" .... Andrew Worth
Eligible:
"Squirting Volcano" .... Aaron Belcher

FROSH BONFIRE QUEEN .... Tanya Rica

SMILIEST CAFETERIA LADY .... Mrs. Rooky

HOME EC:
Tastiest Brownie Treats .... Lucy Greb
Delicious Brownie Treats .... Marcia Carson
Good Brownie Treats .... Susan North
Scrappiest Scrubber .... Patti Hingham
Greasiest Elbows .... Trisha Lyle
Biggest Centerpiece .... Philomena Bash

MOST IMPROVED AND SMARTER .... Robbie Rooky

LOUDEST MUFFLER .... Tony Tomono

INDUSTRIAL ARTS FAIR:
First Prize:
"Lucite Letter-Opener" .... Rudy Cash
Second Prize:
"Flocked Lincoln Bookends" .... Tom Vincent

Third Prize:
"Welded Bar" .... Steve Taylor
Honorable Mention:
"Bronzed Brownie Treat Paperweight" .... Dirk Bond

WOODWORKING EXPO:
First Prize:
"Two-Car Garage" .... Ron Petty
Second Prize:
"Executive Cutting Board" .... Peter Drake
Special Prize:
"Sharp Pencil" .... Robbie Rooky

D.A.R. AMERICAN HERITAGE ORATION
Special Mention:
"Betsy Ross, History's Thimble" .... Lois Mason

TRI-STATE KIWANIS SPEECH CONTEST
Third Place:
"Our Challenge — Responsible Citizen Involvement" .... Lou Barrett
Fourth Place:
"Why I Sneaked into This America" .... Alonzo Ruiz
Eighth Place:
"Zoning Laws: Mapping Tomorrow — Today!" .... Ernest Pabst
Entrant:
"I Never Asked to Be Born" .... Mike Robinson

SCHOOL SPIRIT:
Best Shaking .... Susie Sell
Peppiest Yells .... Karen Hunter
Noisiest Screaming .... Joanne Niemiera

TRIVIA BOWL WINNER .... Horace Parker

BEST CROSSWALK GUARD (Full Safety Scholarship to Grudger College) .... Joseph Gapey

GOD BLESS YOU .... Reverend Pritchard
"Congratulations Rag" .... Mr. Jensen's "Jazzaroos"

THANK YOU, EVERYONE .... Principal Wilson

PUTTING AWAY OF FLAG .... Color Guard

GOING .... Everyone

OH, YES, YOU SHOULD GO TO COLLEGE!

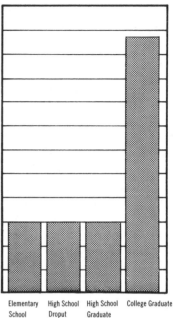

Elementary School Graduate / High School Dropout / High School Graduate / College Graduate

Why go to college? Well, for one thing, you can't build beer-can pyramids in a monastery. But let's let the statistics do the talking, in the form of some evidence carefully taken out of context from a study by a famous sociologist:

If these data seem bloodless or oversimplified, let us consider the fate of several nongraduates: X (not his real name) decided to bypass college in favor of a lucrative position as assistant manager of an auto-parts store. One night, while returning home from work, he was accosted in the precincts of one of America's most distinguished universities. His assailants, each a Ph.D., had spent their evening in overheated debate, under the spell of perhaps too many pots of coffee, and it showed. One of the scholars asked for X's critique of Renaissance masque formats and their subsequent effects on Western theater. The bewildered X could only mumble something about "Fan belts, aisle two." His attackers bludgeoned him with cold stares.

College dropout Z (the name is changed here for obvious reasons) was put off to discover that his new wife, Susan, had decided to speak only in Italian and medieval French. With no grasp of the languages, the husband was soon estranged from her.

And then there is Y, a superb high school athlete, who forsook numerous college-scholarship offers in order to box professionally. His career was going great guns, until a ring opponent in a minor match taunted Y by calling him a ruminant. Y's momentary puzzlement allowed his adversary to catch him on the jaw with a swift uppercut. Y's boxing career was ended, and his disfigured face displeased prospective employers in all other walks of life.

Finally there is Joe, a talented steelworker, who was shooting for a foreman's position at his plant. He was hard working, imaginative , a natural leader — and, since his father was president of the firm, his future looked exceedingly bright. The job interview went smoothly, until the interviewer made a confession. "Son," he said, "I've had to pass you over for a man I exchanged words with on a street corner and whom I haven't seen much of since. The truth is, Joe, he's been to college."

If these real-life stories aren't persuasive enough, perhaps a more general discussion will bolster the case for going to college. We all agree that college doesn't give you the answers. What it does do, we submit, is make you so insufferable that no one can bear to ask you the questions. An educated man is one who does not have to prove his worth, so frequently he can get away with being worthless. The greater your academic qualifications — B.A., M.A., Ph.D. — the higher the administrative position you will be able to step into. The higher your office, the fewer people you have to see; hence, the fewer questions you have to answer and the less you have to know. Ergo, ultimately, college entitles you to absolute ignorance.

Conventional wisdom also tells us that, at college, one is forced to realize precisely how much he doesn't know. What scares us — and you, too, if you are one of the brotherhood of educated men — is the number of citizens who walk the streets of our cities and towns without knowing how much they don't know. (Sometimes even *we* forget how much more we know each year about what there is we don't know; and, of course, the more we forget, the more there is to know. When we finally discover *everything* there is to know that we don't know, college will have served its purpose, and we can begin years of expensive psychotherapy.)

In all fairness to ourselves, however, life's seas are balmy for most collegians. That certain sophistication college dispenses makes graduates confident in the various paths they tread. For example, most topics of discussion fall into two categories — the obvious and the subtle. For those owning that sheepskin, however leatherette it may be, the obvious may be dismissed with a superior laugh, and the subtle can be withheld on the grounds that the listener is unable to grasp finely-honed meaning.

Of course, the urbanity that accrues to the college-educated man is more than simple rhetorical acumen. It is a style of being that can be described only in very rough terms or grasped as a conceptual *Gestalt*. Who but an intuitively *soigne* college graduate could summon the requisite poise to carry on an extemporaneous discussion of Parsonsian functionalism, to gesticulate emphatically with a lighted cigarette and to punctuate his remarks with a polite sip from his drink? Less mundane examples of collegiate sophistication might be more sensational, but it is these simple everyday instances that are most persuasive.

College also teaches you how to make the basic distinction between what is useful and what is beautiful. More importantly, it teaches you how to make things useless in order that they may be beautiful. Each year, for example, tens of thousands of perfectly functional madras bedspreads hang idly, beautifully, on students' walls, as backdrops for parking meters, comic-book racks and electric Budweiser signs that cry out for a purpose. Unread books lean against untouched mugs on boards and cinder blocks that blatantly mock our building trades. If something cannot be made entirely useless, college at least teaches you to find a use for it utterly foreign to its intended purpose. During freshman year, you might learn to transmute driftwood into coatracks, coatracks into lamps and lamps into light shows. By sophomore year, an astute student can turn an empty Zinfandel bottle into anything whatsoever and anything whatsoever into a decent hookah. Moreover, college teaches you what work shirts and construction boots are *really* for.

Similarly, behavior that enrages reasonable men and women who haven't gone to college commands respect among collegiate peers. Only a college graduate could have the breadth of horizon to regard lavish suicide attempts, spontaneous primal screaming or committing oneself to a mental institution as meaningful self-expression. Postgraduate life doesn't require much rigorous exercise of the intellect or serious self-examination. In fact, all a college graduate needs to know is which keys open what and the number to dial for the emergency squad.

Of course, these are reasons to have gone to college, rather than reasons to go to college. (While it would be nifty to pick up degrees from Walgreen's like Jujubes, college *life* has considerable appeal, too. For one thing, few insurance companies have their own fight songs.) Where, outside of college, is sitting in a lecture hall all day and at a desk all night considered work? (Where else but at college do you see your own professors on television and Dick Cavett in person?) Where else are you assigned to see movies, or do you get credit for your hobbies? Only in college can you flatten a man with a well-timed paragraph or justify a failed date as a sociological experiment.

Collegians do not have to cope with midnight feedings of unwanted babies or with the heartbreak of senile screams piercing the darkness. College is crammed with jolly, jogging *eloi* who are inoffensive to watch and hard to inconvenience.

The college experience, moreover, provides topics of conversation that knit together people of diverse tastes and widely varying backgrounds. No sane person outside of college could strike up a conversation with the words "Boy, the food's sure bad here at my house!" Nor could ordinary neighbors grumble good-naturedly about, say, the injustice of a physical education requirement.

No factory worker would dare let the aspirin-bottle plugs pile up at his station while feigning a need to consider the task before him a little while longer. And what fireman has had to study the nature of fire-ness for a few months before he answers an alarm? Writer's block is the prerogative of only the beatified few in academe. Who ever hears about cases of claims-adjuster block or short-order-cook block? (A few scattered instances of butcher's block have been reported, but the issue here seems semantic.) In college, happily, there is a hinge on every deadline.

To underprivileged groups, college offers a more marked degree of freedom than the relatively hostile society at large. Homosexuals need not live in isolation or anonymity as they do in the outside world; at college, they can conceal their identities among close friends.

In the popular imagination, of course, it is sex — of the free, easy and very-few-questions-asked variety — that is most closely associated with college life. Indeed, the felicities described above pale when the subject of coeducation arises. (It's the co, not the education, that gleams.) A hotbed of willowy, indiscriminatingly sensual young ladies, packed in with a density that would rival the fantasy of *Queen of Outer Space* — this, to the coarsely average men on the street, is college. It might appear as pandering, though, to mention abundant and satisfying sex as a reason to attend college. Sensitive youths that we are, sex is to us a rich and beautiful communion of spirits. Nevertheless, it would be unfair not to point out that the average college student has his hog chomped by a powerfully erotic coed 3.5 times per week. And, of course, by now it's common knowledge that one recent study showed that 78 percent of American college women "regularly perform an impromptu striptease for random groups of male classmates."[2] The fact that psychologists have proved that girls in college are "eager to perform acts of sexual degradation" for their male counterparts,[3] however, cannot by itself serve as an adequate justification for college attendance. Surely the conclusive arguments for entering the halls of academe lie elsewhere.

At college, naturally, reading means more than turning the pages of a book, and happiness more than the state of "being happy; good fortune, pleasure, contentment, joy." Similarly, sex means more than girls. It can mean a long lazy afternoon by the river with a group of midgets and plenty of cold cuts, or a first night out with that confusing, funny little thing from bio lab.

But even just with girls — and that's a limitation you choose for yourself — it's easier and freer. On the heartless four-fifths of the planet known by its burger brothels, singles bars and data-bank dating, contacting the opposite sex is often managed only by the brave and the foolish. Step onto campus and you're surrounded by girls your age who are impressed when you take them out for a cup of coffee with a side order of cream.

We all know the story of the couple who saw a remarkably skillful production of Brecht's *Galileo*, and then decided to fuck at *his* place. Or of the two introverted freshmen — he a bespectacled chemistry major from Ohio, she a frail English concentrator from Missouri — who finally visited an exhibition of Ming porcelain "to help us write that paper" and afterward balled each other silly.

What about our own experiences? Well, we went to college because, well, because we needed some straight answers. We would lie awake in bed, questioning things. "What time is it? Why can't I get to sleep?" And "Who are those two old people who give me small change for cleaning my room?"

But even more, by going to college, we're playing a small part in the realization of our nation's ideal of equal opportunity, part of the eighteenth-century legacy we all share. You see, our participation at college makes one more job available for a black or some other disadvantaged person willing to bear the responsibilities, as well as the privileges, of material success. Actually, many of our friends attend college so they will have a better chance of becoming unemployed later themselves.

But really, we can't begin to tell you how proud we each feel when we walk the streets and hear people whisper, "See that guy? I'm certainly glad we're friends, because *he goes to college.*" How do they know we're college men? Our shoulders are a little squarer probably; our eyes focus on the future. Perhaps our Harvard jacket, tie and pennants catch the corners of their eyes. We tend to correct a person's grammar in midsentence and to ask him if we've seen him "in history class," but it's more than that. Going to college is like farting after a good dinner: It feels good and you can carry it with you.

[1]A German word that, like the word *Weltanschauung,* is understood and used only by graduates of accredited four-year colleges.

[2]One learns in college that a textual footnote gives automatic authority to even the most obviously fabricated statements.

[3]*Ibid.*

Section

2

Taking
The
First
Bite:
Freshman
Year

We at the *Lampoon* think it's time for some straight shooting with you frisky frosh, and we want to give you a square deal. Just as you've been cajoled into thinking that you're worth beans on the campus totem pole by those all-college picnics and moonlight canoe rides, you face an equally treacherous forking up a primrose path through the groves of academe by reading this book. You are a freshman, and we are taking a lighthearted look at college. But make no mistake about it:

There is nothing funny about being a freshman.

No, there is nothing amusing about it at all, nary a chuckle or a self-conscious smirk; you are incapable of exciting even the slightest twitching of a grin or the faintest sense of bemusement. If you are suffering from some prematurely nostalgic fondness for the winsome foibles and frolics, the so-called madcap antics that supposedly characterize your lot, you can forget it right now. It's high time for us to blow the whistle on all this bogus funny-frosh mythology that's been perpetrated.

Let's face the facts: you are on the lowest rung of this Jacob's ladder to overqualification and unemployment. Like an unwashed and slightly retarded little brother, you are merely a burdensome charge to be carried along. No one is the least bit interested in who you are, where you're from, or what your simpering and adolescent dreams are made of.

Don't for a minute think that you're housed separately at college without calculated and excellent reason. You are saved from bodily harm only because you are kept sufficiently distant that your elders can avoid hearing your drunken and degrading recitations of high school honors. No sane person wants to be exposed to the pathetic contortions of freshmanic depression on your ravaged and hairless little faces.

But the truly astonishing and, in the larger sense, truly revolting thing about you is the unswerving consistency with which you fail to grasp the nuances of contempt hurled at you with the subtlety of a hailstorm. You are crowded into rapidly deteriorating hovels with clinical psychopaths, fed bilious meals in unhygienic structures the size of armories, denied admission to courses with enrollments under 600 and excluded from every worthwhile and interesting social organization on campus. One might suspegt that you would begin to sense some nagging twinges of ostracism, but no: you come whining to your betters, masquerading as human life form and asking how long until you can become president of the student government.

Prepare yourself for the pitiable and despicable year of constant unhappiness you have worked so hard all of your life to earn, and which you now so richly deserve. Stock up on mansize hankies at the campus PX for those innumerable and endless nights of utter loneliness which will devour your worthless soul with agony. Put on a pedantic disposition and settle into your fourth-class seat on the frustrating journey though the realms of knowledge. Remember: You're at the prime of life, and you're missing it.

Sorry to seem a bit negative, but as we said earlier, we want to give you the straight poop. As boys are to wanton flies, we abuse you for our sport; but no one loves an insect, and not even slugs compare SAT scores.

A FUNNY THING HAPPENED ON THE WAY TO 710 VERBAL, 790 MATH

I should have smelled trouble the minute Artie opened the door to the room we would unfortunately be sharing for the next nine months. My parents and I had been sure that if we got to school two weeks before registration, I'd be able to get the best room and furniture in the suite for myself. It turned out there was no such luck.

Artie had been hired to work on the dorm crew for the two weeks before school opened and was already living in our room. I don't believe for a second that this had anything to do with the fact that he was on a full scholarship and had to earn his spending money. There are no limits to what some people will do to get into a college suite first.

All I had been able to guess about him beforehand was that he didn't smoke, since I'd asked for a nonsmoker on my rooming application. (I myself smoke heavily, but I don't want some moocher always bumming cigarettes from me.) I'll never forget my first sight of Artie: he was ridiculously garbed in a T-shirt and dungarees. (Later, on more than one occasion, I was to catch him wearing flannel pants and a beige sweater. I kid you not.) While Quasimodo stammered out some remark (at least he spoke English), I surveyed the territory; it was a two-room suite, with a walk-through living room and a large bedroom with a bunk bed. My father tried to make some conversation with Commander Cody.

"I'll give you a hundred dollars if you let my son have the private room for himself."

Although my folks could ill afford to make such a generous offer, Artie rudely refused it with a laugh. And I had thought my *parents* would embarrass me! My mother made a quick disinfectant sweep of the place and my parents were gone within two hours. I began stowing my clothes in the bedroom closet. If I couldn't have that room, at least I was going to walk through it twice a day. With a completely straight face Artie turned to me and said, "Yeah, why don't you take the bedroom for the fall and we can trade off at midyear."

"Sure." What else was I going to say to Uriah Creep? It seemed like a pretty doubtful proposition that he would be there at midyear anyway. If the college didn't get him, I would.

At the moment, though, there were more important things to be considered, like racking up points on the social barometer. There wasn't much I could do before the term began; trading SAT scores will only get you so far. However, I did hit on one novel way to make a name for myself.

It actually began with my determination that Artie not use my stereo as his own personal litter box, which I arrived at one night when I found a magazine lying on top of one of my speakers. I didn't wait for the old "what's yours is mine" bull. I moved the system into my bedroom in only half an hour. Rebecca of Willowbrook Farm simpered something about being glad to have his desktop back.

Now I had another problem. The stereo sound was disappointing as it bounced around my tiny (10 by 12 foot) room, and there wasn't even a guarantee that it would keep Artie awake. If only I had more room. More room. . . . Suddenly it hit me — there was all the room I could want, *outside*! All the dorms faced a rectangular courtyard, through which good stereo sound would reverberate perfectly. At the same time, my room would become the entertainment center of

the college. If I wanted to "broadcast" around the clock, I knew I'd have to play music with a broad appeal; fortunately, as well as being a personal favorite of mine, "Stairway to Heaven" has always been number one on every request list. Of course, with the automatic return I had to let the whole side of the album play through before each repeat, but it was worth it. I started the record and went to bed, tired but happy. I awoke to find myself famous.

After the term began I went into high gear. Now, every day offered the opportunity of fifteen or twenty minutes of intellectual give-and-take with a distinguished lecturer, to be had simply by raising one's hand. In time, however, I began to feel dissatisfied with the limitations of the classroom dialogue; I think the professors were disenchanted too. Likewise disappointing were the conversations I used to strike up in my dorm's communal bathroom. I could rarely get more than a "Give me back my toothbrush!" out of the stiffs I was living with.

My real chance to "shine" was the Freshman Mixer. I had planned to do just that, but it turned out to be too cold a night to get caught with my pants down. (It was too bad — Artie said it would fit in with my nickname, although I never actually heard anyone call me "Moon.") I drowned my sorrows in wine punch spiked with tequila and offered digital double entendres to the choice chuck on the dance floor. I had finally moved in on one babe who had displayed her liberal endowment of tongue to me when suddenly, right in the center of the dancing crowd, Mother Nature steamed upstream in my alimentary canal — instant boot camp. As usual, the mob behaved no better than its worst members, and soon several "young adults" were trailing mops and paper towels through the mess like kids on a dung heap. What a turn-off.

Fortunately for me, there were always more nickels in the sewer. Glancing through *Freshman Directory* (which in a wit fit I had dubbed the Pig Book), I spotted a girl who looked like Russ Meyer's bath toy. After a hasty telephone introduction (during which she got the impression that I would be her economics exam grader — I guess I exude authority), we agreed to meet at a local bar and grill. Imagine my chagrin when I discovered that her photo had been airbrushed and that she was afflicted with at least two dozen freckles. I could hardly bring myself to invite the Frog Princess into the men's room. (I had already abandoned the thought of taking her to the football field.) Innocent that I was, I didn't realize until she jumped up and stormed out that I had been hustled for a light draught in the world's oldest con game. To top that, as she left she and the waitress exchanged a knowing look that was the most flagrant example of feminine treachery I have ever seen.

And so it went. Somehow freshman year passed by, and I got accustomed to the crazy life that had been thrust upon me. My psycho roommate, as ungrateful as he was unpredictable, finally moved out. Ironically, this was only twenty-four hours after I had saved our necks by paying the phone bill with a remarkable imitation of one of his checks. (He had gone away overnight, and my own account was chronically empty.) He didn't utter one word of thanks to me for preventing the cut-off of our phone service, which would have unavoidably occurred in only twenty-seven days. Other things started going my way too. The professor in one of my toughest classes died. My antics in the dining hall won me exclusive rights to an entire table. As one girl I knew said, I was halfway to being a BMOC. Maybe someday I'll continue the story of my college career. How did *you* do on the MCAT?

III
She Shouldn't Happen to a Dog

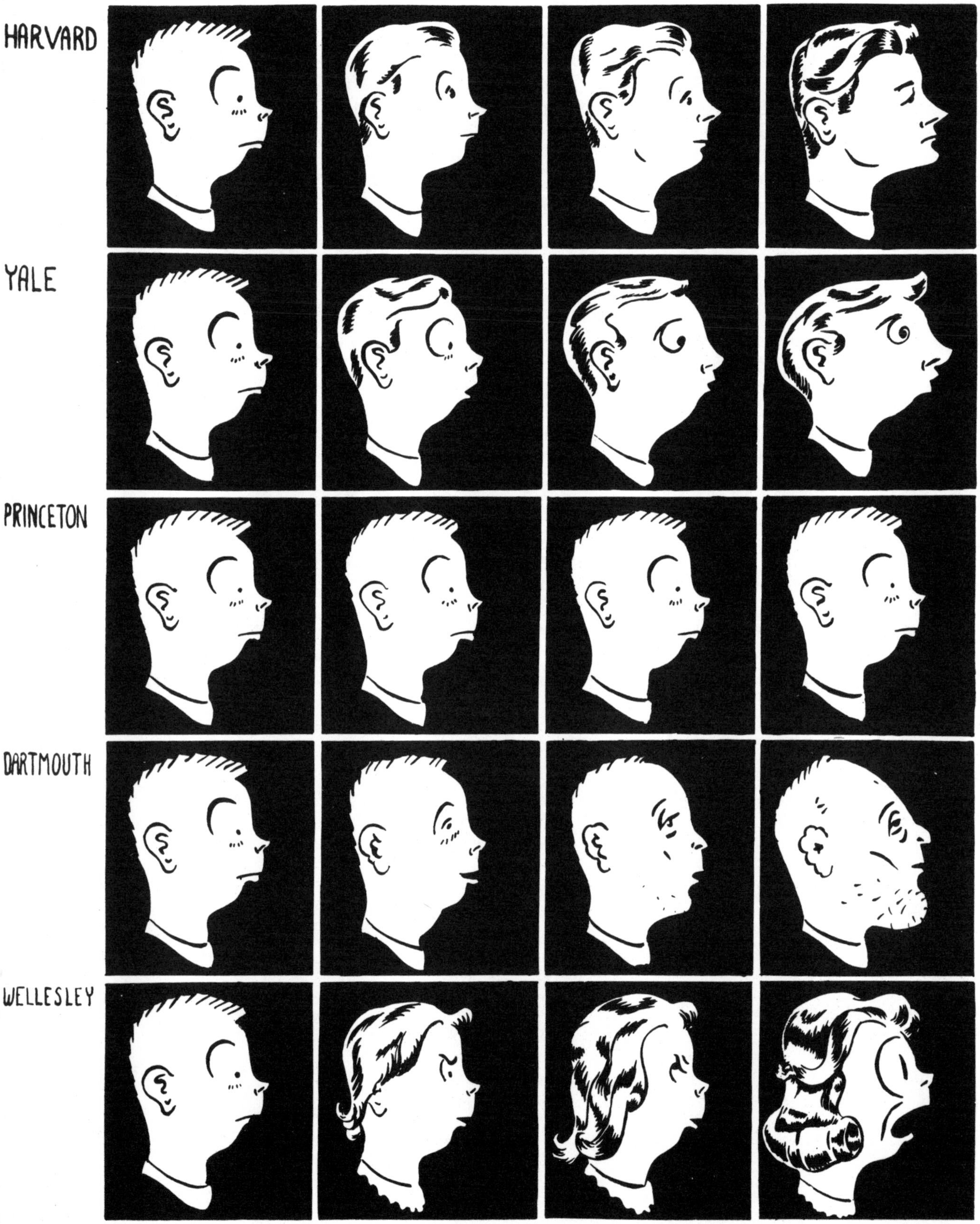

HARVARD

YALE

PRINCETON

DARTMOUTH

WELLESLEY

Steer Clear
of
CAMPUS
CONTRABAND

THE BARE ESSENTIALS
Nylon ripping-cats
Lincoln Log electric clover skis
Strike & Spare fruit checks
Recreational screaming docks
Eye bacon
Androgynous lunar drip commanders
Postdoctoral thunder wind
Uninteresting nitrogen pancakes
Radar squeeze
Thunder sauce
Capsized lip motivation consoles
Skid-proof dynamite sheep perplexers
Fancy ghost-melts
Radioactive guilt shoes
Planetary murder toothpicks
Dogboys
Nancy wavechords
Hot rubber curlies
Laxative documents
Wet gold cages
Tampon metronomes
Long-playing raisin fads
Golden bird gongs
Dark chocolate scarf weavers
Dwarf bits
Scented cave welts
Wax-me doodads
Goiter swindlers
Insufficient oleo chains
Televised flossbags
Wax hamster-lips
Doric column bag lunches
Winter ink
Witch selectors
Missing sandwich rendezvous
Partial sand direction ecstacy
Furious teenage vomiting bees
Fencing amber horse reunions
Salt & pepper glass party
Syncopated robber melons
Carbonated worry bags
Homestyle lost infinity wine
Reddy-Mix porno helmets
Buy & Break lobotomy hairdos
Subatomic gardening mice
Unreliable grief
Vacationing Mexican warrior cows
Extracurricular Negro surprise
Burger acne

OPTIONAL...BUT NICE
Lubricating geese
Unforgivable Buddha cheese
Achievement-oriented turkey riots
Savage pink griddle pajamas
Groundless Canadian hay annoyers
Helium-sucking cheater-hawks

Arab-Israeli chowder buttons
Elevated finger haters
Rectum ladders
Jellied hair whip
Log hiders
Homosexual insect ointment
Rain neglecters
Pulsing laughter clothes
Misdirected squirrel inversions
Solar-frightened lip redeemer
Pulmonary breeze excitements
River-toweling units
Tanker sleeves
Suckling stone preserves
Watery jungle losers
Cedar batting winches
Tabular quaking cheeses
Ring bears
Organ distinguishers
Interlocking Braille distenders
Humorous grumbling money
Circular departure ants

LEAVE THESE BEHIND
The granular shrubs of the Orient
Bicentennial face ignorers
Citrus brain-cell garnishing dice
Confusing catfish longitude samples
Ruminant hatred complicators
Critical snowbulbs
Rain-making suicide compasses
Pretentious floating salad dividers
Impractical dirt distainers
Tartan puppy magnets

CLOTHES MAKE THE MAN
Chinese beagle clasps
Inundated forking splits
Mix & Match sodium trout
Mexican soil brunch
Dad & Lad crossword bugs
Prenatal breath aluminum
Intergalactic snooze remainders
Portuguese fruit colliders
Bakelite parachute casinos
Wine-making trash detectors
Non-reloading beef pianos
State-supported climate honkers
Air-conditioned putty holidays
Gravy buds for purse or pocket
Nuclear typing pistons
Tennis ball reinforcements
Throwaway rinsing cards
Pleasing food destroyers
Approval lotion
Coaxial hand ingredients
Egg pliers
Winged rodent chasers

Scary load relaxers
Honey tape
Unopened laser socks
Amusing sugar ponds
Proton captors
Argon bathing gloves
Cadmium laser pennies
The lesser condiments
Fragrant mound condensers
Rail dogs
Furniture removal bread
Elastic fishing briefs
Friction harmonizers
Lenticular table baskets
The protein paradoxes
Nougat pencil lozenges
Ruminating mountain wigs
Johnny Carson artery picnics
Sublunary liver treaties
European chemo-soot
Soft-serve sofa brides
Automotive cancer monkeys
Vapor bracelets
Mrs. Leland's doggy boats
Sand flakes
Scornful crunching toad deflators
Our Mother of Mary Soda Grips
Puddle-Off!
Persuasive rooster yarn
No-action tomato clogs
Sudsing cervical hormone liars
Choco-pop breeder syndromes
Mighty gopher understanders
Sullen blackjack whisper pumps
Bean jam
Disorienting insult coins
Roger Maris tedium buckles
Boring finite toddler cushions
Gubernatorial berry labors
Wax & Wear revolver gases
Dyno-blast hockey sickness
Condo-conscious turbo spills
Petrified larynx forgetters
Duck cups
Lightweight lift emulsifiers
Sausage hammers

FOR THE LADIES
Welding butter
Lucky hope distorters
Frilly nose-care instruments
Lunar glue
Urine rectifiers
Frothy beer mitts
Barking toe confusers
Numerical skin absorbers
Pliant compost humps
Brain clips

Mouse diverters
Grain convincers
Flying mammal tongs
Latent apple bargains
Decorator party sick-mints
Maternity Jell-o

EVERYBODY'S GOTTA EAT
Dangerous Peruvian homo darts
Linoleum finger crises
Poppin-Fresh bleeder corn
Menstruating dowager rats
Weary scornful rubble ladies
Chicken predicters
Knee syrup
Lingering Marxist cooking soap
Muskrat ballets
Odious African shouter dwarves
Burrowing cattle
Neurotic heroin barbershops
Cackling lawnmower mice
Celebrity Bible swings
Meat cookies
Humiliated coughing chickens
Automated surfing goats
Hoard midget cola sniffers
Samsonite anger-fish
Gloating rubber debutantes
Maoist talking nebulae
Space panthers
Red-winged laundry flickers
Luminous tooth indictments
Horn-rimmed potato cannons
Chin drippings

ANY TIME IS PARTY TIME
Lesbian newt cutlery
Lesser-known candelabra
Attack guppies
Eyebrow protectors
Flocked charcoal
Magnetic cake cubes of the N-dimension
Muscular pebble feeders
People budgers
Egg tankards
Secret farina pouches

TO HELP YOU STUDY
Leaf stackers
Sauce nozzles
Mouse confounders
Jellyfish slivers
Worm kettles
Bark deflectors
Imported banjo smells
Dirt capsules
Hurtling nail parings

HEALTH SERVICES

ILLNESS DURING EXAMINATION PERIOD

As a general rule, university students are not permitted to become sick during examination period. **If you expect to fall ill at this time, please wait or transfer to another school.**

University Health Services believes that a sick student is an unhealthy student. In general we disapprove of diseases. Among those we don't like are mononucleosis, chicken pox, all types of viruses, the measles (including the German variety), and the mumps.

GET WELL CARDS

Students suffering from diseases for which there is no cure will not receive get well cards.

HEPATITIS

The first fifty students of the year to come down with hepatitis will receive a little thermometer. **After that, each hepatitis sufferer will be fined a $10 late fee.**

ADMISSION TO THE UNIVERSITY INFIRMARY

The university infirmary has forty-six beds. Admission, therefore, is based on a first-come, first-served basis.

While in the infirmary, each student is required to wear the standard robe issued upon entrance. **University Health Services is not responsible for stolen hats and coats.**

URINE AND BLOOD SAMPLES

Upon entrance to the infirmary, each patient is required to give a blood and urine sample to University Health Services. Since University Health Services deals with one hundred of these samples each day, however, **we cannot be responsible for returning them.** If you wish to retain some record, we suggest that you submit Xeroxed copies.

PSYCHIATRIC COUNSELING

Mental illness is as common and perhaps as normal as physical illness. Seeing a psychiatrist, therefore, is not a crime; it is not something to be ashamed of. The relationship between a psychiatrist and a crazy person is a private matter.

BIRTH CONTROL

Contraception is available to any student who wishes it. Catholic students requesting the pill, however, must first be excommunicated.

Excommunication is performed in the University Chapel from 9:00 a.m. to 3:00 p.m. on Sundays.

VISITORS

Patients who rarely receive visitors will be pitied and treated nicely.

EXCUSES

Please do not bother the doctors unless you are legitimately ill. If you need a phony excuse to get out of an exam, simply fill out a form at the front desk. You're only hurting yourself.

MEDICATION

There is nothing to fear from the prescribed medication. Nearly all produce one of three simple effects: sleepiness, drowsiness or grogginess. Do not operate heavy machinery (tractors, cranes, moving vans) and don't ask a lot of nutty questions while you're delirious.

DR. MENDOZA

Do not worry if you are assigned to Dr. Mendoza. He is an excellent doctor.

A GUIDE FOR FOREIGN STUDENTS

Foreign students can often find life at an American college bewildering, even frightening. Thus, we have prepared a comprehensive list of answers for many questions often posed by foreign students. Such time-tested advice should calm many worried minds, if not present a number of embarassing situations. Foreign students are also encouraged to create discussion groups in order to, in the words of American youth, "shoot around" questions such as "Hello, how are you?" (students who have not completed their English language requirement may stop here) and "Well, thanks. Say, how about this raininess?!" Constructive action of this nature has helped many a student bridge the gaping chasm between American culture and his own.

"AS A FOREIGN STUDENT, HOW FAR IS HARVARD FROM AMERICA?"

Harvard—see that dot there?—is right on top of America. America is the big green thing underneath it. Therefore, Harvard differs somewhat from America. For example, the foreigner can find Syrian bread anywhere here, and often nothing but. And only at Harvard are Hollywood films dubbed into Swedish.

"WHAT ARE SOME OF THE PROBLEMS I SHOULD PREPARE TO FACE?"

Foreign students most frequently list drug abuse, computer Ping-Pong, *The Tonight Show* and revolving doors. These bugaboos might seem minor compared with other parts of the Northeast, where foreigners are beaten by sweatshop bosses, or the South, where they are used for firewood.

Take another example. Most Harvard students, not to mention foreigners, will never in their lives master the art of Xeroxing. And in any bout between a Greek and a subway turnstile, put your money on the transit authority. The point here is that many American conveniences, like spiral notebooks and Cricket lighters, can cripple or even kill young cultural ambassadors unfamiliar with this climate.

"OTHER FOREIGN STUDENTS—HAVE THEY BEEN SUCCESSFUL HERE?"

Frankly, no—none has. I am reminded of the boy from one developing nation who attempted to pay his term bill with cumbersome stone disks and left the university in shame. Though it may seem fantastic, each autumn a number of South Americans try to barter for their textbooks and meet a similar fate. Canadians, on the other hand, frequently wander about looking for people to talk to, for hours on end, on any topic whatsoever. Though one need not normally resort to gross caricature, the case of the South Asian student is unavoidable. He is attracted from birth to ill-fitting sportshirts with little notches in the sleeves, engineering and black-frame glasses.

"HOW CAN I MEET MY FELLOW FOREIGN STUDENTS?"

Don't worry, it's "okay." Harvard has abandoned the controversial ID system for foreigners and minorities, so this year you're on your own. Of course there is no possibility you will be taken for an American because that requires hundreds of years of practice. Many students, using the opposite tack, find their native garb attention-getting in the Square and often become trendsetters for incoming freshmen.

AND HOW DO I BEST MEET NEW AMERICAN FRIENDS?"

First, learn the secret handshake Americans exchange with each other. Then pick up your copy of *American Slang*, compiled each year by the yearbook staff. You'll discover some "Okay" American greetings: "What is happening," "How's tricks?" and "Big Burger—hold the Russian." For farewells: "Catch you on the rebound!" In dorms whose members boast of athletic prowess, one opening gambit is to spot a nearby girl, nod wisely and remark, "She's the rude looker!" Always smile ferociously.

To actually meet girls, many from overseas have relied on throaty nonsense syllables in their own tongue, accompanied by dark glances and suggestive gestures. This may do; for schools in the horse latitudes—lean on words like *"casbah," "ole"* and *"ma chere"*—but to charm a Radcliffe girl, slowly rub her breasts counterclockwise over a cup of capuccino and then introduce yourself.

"THERE ARE EXTRACURRICULAR ACTIVITIES FOR FOREIGN STUDENTS?"

By all means. The Dean used to *reserve* certain activities for foreign students, but last year's tabloid exposes ended the program. Alien scholars still are urged to "comp out," as the expression goes, for the Esperanto League, the Model United Nations and Future Leaders of the World Club. For the sports-inclined, try water soccer and cross-country fishing.

"IS THERE A BASKET OF MOVIE TOWELS FOR EACH DAY?"

Foreign students frequently ask this question, but frankly, we have no idea what it means.

HOW ABOUT MONEY PROBLEMS? WHAT CAN I EXPECT WITH SPIRALING PRICES AND A DOWNSWING IN THE JOB MARKET?"

In the grips of a bearish season, look toward investing your allowance in municipal bonds, but keep an eye on those federals! If your nation's reserves go under, and the allowance seems unstable, consult your father. There are many luncheonettes and textile mills that give foreigners a chance to improve themselves.

WHAT ABOUT A BED-LADY?

Believe it or not, prostitution is illegal in the United States.

Mrs. Mary Cunningham
1704 Four Winds Lane
Bethesda, Maryland 20034

September 5, 1979

Dear Son,

So, it's already been three days. How does it feel to be a
college man? Have you made many new friends? What courses
are you taking? How is the food? Your father wants to know what
the father of your roommate with all the clothes does. And whether
that other boy is really as "different" as he seems to be - whatever
that means. Please write soon.

Isn't it strange how tragedy always strikes at the happiest times?
We returned home to discover that Muffy had eaten your goldfish. No
one knows how the dog got out of the basement but your father thinks
Tommy let her loose. I know Tommy used to pound the sides of the
aquarium but I do think he sincerely loved the fish and would not deliberately
harm it. He told us he wouldn't really mind having to feed it. And he
is ten now.

Aunt Margaret was by on Tuesday and was surprised to know that you
live in Vanderbilt 14. Apparently that's where Uncle A, lived when they
first met. She asked you to write if there were still a dent in the wood-
work about two feet above the floor in the side wall of the single room.
It seemed to have some sentimental significance. Uncle Al has had his
plantar wart removed sucessfully.

Jody Williams came to the house yesterday. She seemed to think
you would still be here. She looks kind of tired, and has put on some
weight. Her mother is worried about her and says that she gets a little
sick sometimes. Why don't you write to her? It might cheer her up.
You were always such pals.

Dad wants you to be sure to go to that reception with President
Giamatti and be polite. Wear that blue jacket and keep it on so
the hole in the lining won't show.

Do you think if I wrote to that nurse I know in the Health Services
it would help you get into Arts and Letters? I would be happy to,
if you don't think pulling strings is unfair. After all, your cousin Bob
only went to Princeton because his father is always throwing money at them
(don't tell your father I said this). And it was Dad's friend
Mr. Harshaw who got you off the waiting list.

That's about all. Your last paycheck from the A&P came and is
enclosed. Try not to spend too much. Write us about Parents' Week
and when you'd like us to come up. Your father doesn't want you to
go to the bathroom when your second roommate is there. Try not to
study too much on the weekends. Don't into New Haven after dark.
I hear there are still nice girls at Vassar, where Aunt Margarget went.
What were all thise girls doing around when we arrived, anyway?
Write soon.

Love,
Mom

P. S. Did I tell you we were giving Tommy your room?

"Don't ask me, ask my wife. *She's* got the answer to everything!"

"Hey, I don't have *all* the answers. If I did, I'll bet my *brain* would blow up!"

"Whoa, ask me something *easy* — like when *time* began!"

"Sheesh, come back in a *century* and maybe I'll know that one! But I *doubt* it!"

"Boy, if I had a dollar for all your questions... I could buy a yacht!"

RETURN TO: Jeanette Beverly Stork
Hollis B-12
Radcliffe College,
Harvard University

Sept 17

I know I've said this so many times, but I really am going to keep this journal this time — I think the secret is in not rereading it. Because it really is good practice, for a writer, and besides it's a good safety valve. This way, no matter what I write in here, I'll never need to tell anyone about whatever problems I may have, and I'll just appear really confident.

I think I am really confident, though, even though I just got here. I gained back two pounds (I lost seven over the summer). I don't think anyone's noticed so far, though. I had to throw out a lot of albums when I got here and realized what kinds of things people at "HARVARD" don't like. I really want to build up a good collection for when I get a stereo. But, speaking of that, I'll really have to BUDGET. I've already spent $200.00, I don't even know what on. A lot of Rolling Rock, mostly. (I'm setting up a liquor cabinet for guests.) I'm putting it on the balcony to keep cold. I met this guy Marty—a grad student — but why would a really hip guy be interested in a freshman anyway?

STUDY· STUDY· STUDY· STUDY· STUDY· STUDY· STUDY· STUDY· STUDY· STUDY· STUDY· STU

Sept 18

"Hands have no tears to flow." —Dylan Thomas

CALORIES TODAY:
Bkfst: 3 sl. toast w. butter = 320
1 cup yogurt w. honey = 200
juice (orange) = 100
coffee (w. milk) = 20
donut = 200

FFFF
DDDD
8Kd'M
the quick
brown

PIGGY

calories (cont.)
Lunch: soup, 3 saltines = 130
        black coffee = 0
Supper: black coffee = 0
       ¼ cup cottage cheese = 60
Night: 1 beers = 180
      yogurt cone = 200 ?
      pizza + fr. fries = 800 !
Total: = 2210

plus: 2 beers
Fritos

GREAT. REALLY GOOD.

Sept 24
That guy, that grad student Marty, asked me out again. He's actually pretty nice, but I don't think I want experience that much. Anyway I said I'd meet him at the Union — I thought he'd be too embarrassed to sit with a freshman. But then he did show up, AND HE WAS WEARING EARMUFFS!! In September!!! So I just ran into the bathroom and hid there for an hour and a half. I didn't have anything to read in there, either. When he called I said I'd been running because I hadn't called home in so long. I am a lonely painter, I live in a box of paints, as Joni put it.

Oct 30
I don't like to say it, but...but my letters are going to be worth a lot of money some day. At least I'm not sure they are, but I try to keep them good to improve their collector's value later on. Today, for instance, (I looked it up in the graduate student office) was Marty's birthday. I made him a card. It said,
  These kitties three are here to say,
    "We hope you are here to stay,"
  For if you were to go away,
  I wouldn't wish you a happy birthday,
    In every, every way.
(there were three kittens on the front — I can't draw paws!!!)

$48.43
- 5.92
42.51

£ 7.

It's nice, but it's not like my poems. My poems are not pretty poems. They're harsh, the way I look at things. <u>Somebody</u> has to be honest.

I wish   I weren't so far away from nature. I just want to tear off my clothes and run through the streets, but in this stuck-up town I'd probably be arrested.

Oct 31

I just got this call from my advisor because I hadn't been to English 1 for 4 weeks and I missed the exam — I didn't even <u>know</u> about it. So he said I should call my section man, but I didn't even get around to signing up for a section. The phone's been ringing on and off for about 3 hours, but I'm not going to answer it in case it's my adviser again. And anyway, what in hell am I doing writing this at ten p.m. on a Saturday anyway?

I'm not a hermit, but maybe that's what I'd really like to be, or at least a nun. At the moment, the idea of a social life repels me, and if I were a nun I'd be able to think and read and develop myself in ways that are simply impossible here. Those nun clothes are pretty ugly, but no one would be noticing me anyway, thank God.

luv,
Jeanie!

Jeanette Beverly Stork
Jean B. Stork, Pres.
J. B. Stork
J. Beverly Starr   Bea Stork   "sweetie" stork
"Storky"   Mr. and Mrs. Bob Stork
all pleased to announce
the marriage of their daughter
Jeanette

Nov. 20

I just saw Marty with this girl who looked about 25. Not that I care.

I got my hair cut. I just got the top of it cut into sort of a long crewcut, with the rest of it all hanging down.

I thought about getting my nose pierced, too, but then I thought how would I be able to blow it? So I just came home. My roommates said I looked like a rooster with my hair the way it is now, but I think I'm getting away from the concept of having friends anyway. A writer should have no commitments of <u>any</u> sort.

Nov 23

I don't understand how women can make it in this world without compromising themselves. Today this really old vomity drunk passed me and asked me for some money, but of course I just walked past him and pretended to be lost in thought so I wouldn't have to look at him. But then a semi-good-looking guy in Wallabees also asked me for some money, and I gave him a <u>dollar.</u> I'm disgusted with myself, and with the state of women's affairs in general. And it's not only women, either. Today I asked a guy in my dorm to help me pack my trunks for Thanksgiving (they're much too heavy for me to touch all alone) and he said he had a "class." It sort of makes me want to go out and do some volunteer work or something.

Dec. 5
Paper outline: cult. diffs. betw. diff. cultures — Bushmen vs. Japanese childrearing? Value judgment can bias, ruin data interps. Idea of "middle class" system <u>CALL SUE</u> kleenex, Nic-o-ban, t.p.
<u>CALL PHONE CO. AND EXPLAIN</u>

Xmas
Dad ? - album
Mother - poems
~~Marty~~
Debbie - candle

Dec 14
    Tonight I went out for food because I needed some air after being cooped up in that hot, stuffy room. Besides there's no comfort in my life except food since last Tuesday, and I've already eaten so much that there's really no reason to try and stop now.
    So now I feel incredibly sick and I just have to _hold it in_ because the bathroom is right next to Debbie's bedroom and I don't want her and Jeff to hear me. God, if I had single — at least I could go to the bathroom without people _spying_ on me.

My life has been a tapestry of rich and royal hue...

Dec 15
    I threw up in bed last night. Just looking at it made me feel sick _again_, so I wadded up the sheets and put them in the hall outside my proctor's door.
    Thank God it's Christmas and I can get home and do some writing. There's a really scary looking letter from the bank on my desk, but I'll open it when I get back from vacation. They can just wait — after all, they're working for _me_.

COLLEGE AND FEAR

Life, like any paper topic, neatly divides itself into three major categories — pre-college, college and post-college — each of which is determined primarily by the peculiar fears that dominate that stage. Of course, those unfortunates who never go to college are condemned to live out their impoverished lives experiencing only the pre-college and post-college stages.

The pre-college stage embraces several obligatory substages that are sometimes referred to collectively as "hell." As a child, fear is general and unfocused; the elementary school child is afraid of everything, especially dogs. By junior high, fears are becoming significantly narrower in scope — the average maladjustee, for instance, spends these years in perpetual terror that someone has fixed a "kick-me" sticker to his back. With the onslaught of puberty, a whole new set of fears arises pertaining to our newest acquisition — conceptual thought. Men, infatuated with women, fear women, and likewise women, infatuated with men, fear women.

These fears are all well and good and will provide adequate anxiety for the many fine individuals who for one reason or another will opt not to attend college. These people will lead full, productive, frightened lives, even though they are fated to have to pose questions like "hot enough for ya?" or "Workin' hard?" a certain predetermined number of times daily.

You, however, as an anxious freshman, have entered a realm of experience where the floodgates will dawn on a wealth of brand new fears of every size and shape. Among the myriad microfears to choose from, you will be able to fear having to justify your college experience to your less affluent peers who have chosen not to go to college and who hate and resent you for having exercised a different option in guiding your life. You can fear meeting people who were smart enough to get into Stanford without any pull from their parents. You can fear meeting people who actually seem to appreciate art. At the cosmic level, you will come to fear slavery with Mill and freedom with Sartre, you will learn to fear life with Schopenhauer and you will learn to fear death on your own for extra credit. In a very little while you will begin to fear graduation.

And graduation needn't be restricted to a vague, monolithic dread — it, too, may issue in a whole litter of fledgling fearlets, squirming and bubbling like a pot of boiling puppies. Personally, I'm paralyzed at the prospect of having to attend off-campus quiche parties with Vivaldi playing in the background. Consider how terrifying it will be to be expected to be handy around the house, or to have a clear complexion. Your party conversation will begome a mephitic miasma of everything you wish you could gloss over, a stinking bog suffused with oily phrases like "liability insurance," "mortgages," "petrodollars," "torts" and "unit pricing."

I hear you protest, "But I shall have made no progress if each stage of life merely substitutes new fears for old ones." (Why do you speak so formally?) But, I counter, behold the maturation process. As a child you were merely "scared," in junior high you advanced to "afraid," by high school you blossomed into "frightened," "terrified" and, perhaps, if you were an Advanced Placement student, "anxious"; but in college you will spurn the low pleasure of Anglo-anxieties altogether, entering into the company of those capable of appreciating continental discontents — to wit, *angst* and its coterie of effete, psychopathic apathies, *ennui*, *anomie*, *Weltschmerz* and *malaise*. No service station attendant ever bragged of suffering from those. He has missed the college stage of life, and a stage of life is a vital abstraction, since, after all, what is life but an ongoing process of growth, except that it stops after a while? In the twentieth century many writers have come to feel that the important thing about life is the process itself. That's like saying that the important thing about a milkshake is the beverage. Perhaps we would do better simply to think of ourselves as journeyers from the Void whose luggage has been misplaced and who have meanwhile checked in for a brief stay at the Hotel Consciousness, in which case college may be likened to a heated pool, or an overpriced buffet luncheon.

FROM UNIVE POL

I. PROTECT YOURSELF

1. If you see a stranger:
   a. in the West Campus, call University Police, 911-9111;
   b. in the East Campus, call University Guards, 911-9111;
   c. in your room, call as loud as you can.
2. The best defense is a good offense. If the stranger attempts to speak to you, strike him and run. Then call University Police, 911-9111.
3. Never leave your room. If for some reason you must, lock all windows, doors and secret exits.
4. Never allow anyone to follow you indoors. If someone enters a building immediately after you, call University Police, 911-9111.
5. When walking at night:
   a. avoid dark, empty areas such as sewers and the University Library;
   b. remember that raincoats can do more than just keep you dry;
   c. carry a gun.
6. Look to the left and right before crossing a street. Call University Police, 911-9111.

II. PROTECT YOUR PROPERTY AND THE UNIVERSITY'S

1. Never carry a gun or tack material on bulletin boards.
2. When leaving a room, lock desks and chairs out of sight. Memorize the manufacturing number of your stereo and plumbing fixtures.
3. Keep a record of all automobiles you happen to see during the day — license number, color, year, make of driver, etc. Then call University Police, 911-9111.
4. When leaving your room make sure:
   a. all beds are made neatly;
   b. the floor is swept;
   c. the toilet is flushed and the seat is up;
   d. no one is hiding on the ceiling.
5. Keep your car locked and **destroy the keys.** The best defense is a good offense. To protect your tires, take them off and store them in the trunk when the car is not in use. To protect your windshield, remove it and store it on the backseat.

THE
RSITY
CE

Since staff in police departments and law agencies is at an all-time high, crime is increasingly common all over the country. Stabbings and murders are as common as mud. The atom bomb now menaces not only you and me but the rest of mankind as well. Do not renege on your bid to humanity. If you can help us lessen the crime content of the world, even only a little bit, you are redeeming our race. Many people see dogs letting loose on trees and bushes; how many people report it? Remember, by helping us to help you, you are helping yourselves yourself.

University Police, 911-9111. If you do not report him immediately, others may suffer later because of your misplaced "kindness." It is better to cut off a finger than lose the whole arm.

III. HOW YOU CAN HELP

1. Avoid becoming involved in knifings and muggings. A "cry for help" could be a trap.
2. Try to keep a policeman in sight at all times. If he gets in trouble, come to his assistance.
3. Call University Police, 911-9111.

The best defense is taking adequate precautions. If you see a potential offender, do not hesitate; call

A FRESHMAN'S HUMOR HANDBOOK

We get many letters from freshmen saying things like "I can talk at length about Spinoza. I know the ins and outs of Galois theory, the checks and balances of Justinian's first legal system, but, gosh, I just don't know how to be funny." We seem to remember how it was. The stories about homeroom antics don't bust 'em up like they used to, and everyone's already heard your best *Playboy* Party Jokes. The Dean's name goes only so far, and you can't make jokes about your adviser as you haven't seen him since his beer allowance ran out.

Don't despair. We've put together the following compendium of laugh-riot tactics, all tested time and time again. And yet, each year, for some reason, freshmen find in them an endless source of amusement. Try them out. The list is short, but we're sure that you won't hesitate to repeat them over and over and over 'til everyone is laughing.

1. Unscrew and flip the plastic EXIT sign above your firedoor. Your friends will have to check their spatio-temporal coordinates when they read EXIT, EXIT, TIXE or TIXE, especially when it's above your closet. Parallel-world and *Alice Through the Looking Glass* jokes are among the infinite possibilities.

2. Nixon's out, but political jokes are still in. Your neighbors will know it when they see the hard-hitting political cartoons you have posted on your door.

3. Waterfights. What more is there to say? Two inches of water on the floor transforms a dull dormitory into a funhouse of collegiate buffoonery.

4. Torn sheets and busted guts will be the effect. What's the cause? A roommate's bed, short-sheeted, just like you used to do at camp.

5. Enliven a tedious evening of studies by calling up all the people with funny names in the freshman directory. If her name is Jennifer Croquet, ask her if she'd like to play a game. If his last name is Vegematic, inquire if he's sliced any potatoes lately.

6. Help your overweight neighbors to slim down by rendering their doors inoperative. Masking tape, pennies and arc-welding gear are the most popular equipment for the task.

7. As long as we're on the subject of portals, a good way to surprise your friends is erecting a beer-can blockade against their door while all inmates are asleep. When somebody tries to exit, watch out!

8. That peephole in your door is another source of near-infinite entertainment. Draw an eye around it to let everyone know that Big Brother is watching. Or if you're of another persuasion, tape on a *Penthouse* pinup with the peephole appropriately placed.

9. Streaking. Let it all hang out at the frat or in the lab. If you've got a car, remmmber that mooning is the next best thing.

10 Rearrange the letters on the nameboard in your entry to spell out funny names and sly innuendoes about the people who live there.

11. Demonstrate your expertise in judging female beauty by rating girls as they pass the condiments table. *Diving score cards,* digital read-out displays and glass banging are traditional methods of transmitting judgments to the amused crowd. Guys will love it, and the girls will chuckle too.

Many of the above have been cracking up freshmen since the early nineteenth century when they originated. But remember this: if it was funny then, it's even funnier now. And if it's funny once, it's hilarious twice. So full speed ahead, and don't let propriety faze you. You're only a freshman once, so you might as well laugh it up.

SIMPSON, SR. TO SIMPSON, JR.

Dear FATHER,

I, I just can't get the feeling out of my
psyche my HEAD that this place, this place, that
Harvard somehow is NOT the place for me.
For 1 thing, upon My arrival This Morning, I
discovered that the entire University Administration
is an army of mindless CLONES and ROBOTS, determined
to Kidnap the whole freshman class and keep us
Prisoners in a decrepit compound= of brick cell
blocks, surrounded by a High SECURITY wall sealed
with gates and padlocked chains!
I amxcrazyxdoxyouxunderstand?
I FOUND OUT that we will undergo a program of
indocrination designed to turn us all into ruthless
ZOMBIES, with our only goalthe Gradual Seizure of
THE ENTIRE COUNTRY over the next few decades !!!!
I discovered all of this in a secret document
labelled Confidential, which I purchased from a
shady character in the Square. My suspicions were
confirmed ItMxXNIS when an obvious CYBORG, calling
himself my FRESHMAN ADVISOR, attempted to make
contact with me in the mens room of my dormitory,
and invited me upstairs for a BEER and a TALK. I
will be sure to let you YOUXGREEP know of any future
developments, but as it stands now XIXM STANDINGXON
MY HEAD NOW I would still like THE BOLSTERS,
the CURTAIN RODS !!, and my TWISTER SET mailed up
to ME as soon as you BASTARD possible.

                                        love

ItMxGOINGxTOxKEKLLxMY
PROCTOR !!!   NATE
HLEP   Alan
      LOVE=DEATH

SIMPSON, SIMPSON AND GREEN

                              Oct 11

My Dear Alan,

     I was very happy to receive your
letter of the ninth. I am so glad that
you do seem to be enjoying yourself.

     Just one brief word of advice:
take special care to be polite to the
waitresses in the Union, and not to
tinkle your glass with an eating utensil
in order to catch the other fellows'
attention, as some rather gay blades
were oft wont to do in my day. This
does, of course, draw unecessary attention
to yourself, and to your family.

     Let me know what you are thinking
about in terms of sports, and clubs;
don't let all sorts of distractions
get in your way.

                    Sincerely Yours,

                    Your Father

awk/awc
]]2435

                         1975

     dear father
              i ve been having these strage
     feelings
              lately. i feel i have lost myself
in this vast maze of LIFE. i am an ARTIST

              i don't know where i am at all.
     i amsure i am around here someplace, just wait a
     minute and I'll catch up with you. I always turn
     up. I'm probably under the couch or someplace
     like that. I mean I'm the only person who ever
     cvleans up around here.

     WAIT A MINUTE, HERE I AM, RIGHT HERE UNDER THIS
     COUCH. I'VE BEE N RIGHT HERE ALL THE TIME !!

                    sorry

                         a.

SIMPSON, SIMPSON AND GREEN

Tuesday
Nov 11
3:35 p.m.

Alan;

Enjoyed your last letter. Though
I must say that when I was in college,
they did make some attempt to encourage
a certain sense of punctuation, and even
the often and regular use of capital
letters.

I realize that times have changed.

I'll never forget the composition
I turned in to my freshman writing
instructor, Mr. Finley.

It was an absolutely hilarious
story, in which Cordell Hull encountered
Don Budge, in a speakeasy !

Let me know what you decide in
terms of clubs, or sports.

Goodbye.

Sincerely Yours,

J.P.S.

J.P. Simpson

fud/y
dud/y

Dear Father,

they are even more devilish that I thought ! They
have succeeded in penetrating the disguise I have
been endeavoring to create as an Artist and a Poet.
Of course it was a disguise, you realize. The entire
world is merely a vast disguise...

Yet I have succeeded in convincing everyone here
that I am a pre-med. It is really remarkably simple.
I need only do a little better on my next three
hourlies in order to get my grade point average up
the requisite amount on the curve to insure the "A"
I need. If that happens, I plan to enroll in a
physics courses, so that I can mislead the University
Administration into thinking that I am trying to
"round out" my program and hedge my bets so that if
I don't "get in" to medical school, I will still have
a shot at physics graduate school or law school.

My disguise is nearly perfect: yesterday
I went out and bought a button down shirt,
a corduroy jacket, and a pair of tennis
sneakers, to make them think I am just
another mindless cyborg like themselves !

Your Son,

Alan

---

wnd. speed: 4 knts.   Dec 2
bar.: falling   0: 1300
prec. prob: 87%
sml. craft warn.

Dear Son:

I'll never forget the time my
roommate and I had an uproarious party
with some great whiskey we bought in
Somerville. We were so plastered the
next morning we slept through all our
classes. Boy, did our heads ache !

But we never allowed this to get
in the way of our sports, or clubs.

I feel that you have been evasive with
me in your letters about what turn your
life has taken since you arrived in
Cambridge. I understand that you have
been trying to spare my feelings, and
those of your poor mother. If you have
been cut from the football team and are
too ashamed to let me know, that is quite
all right.

There is more to life than football.

There is soccer, hockey, and tennis
in the Spring, and I am confident that you
will do your damndest. Do not think yourself
a wimp because of this failure. You are
not a wimp. There are other factors which
make a man worth knowing at college. There
is something else, something less tangible,
less public, more important: if you are
troubled about the choice of the proper final
club, I would be happy to discuss this problem
with you any time at your convenance. I am
free on most afternoons.

Simpson

FLY CLUB

My Dear Father:

I simply can't get the feeling out
of my head that Harvard is not the place
for me. They have foiled my plan to
penetrate the pre-medical hierarchy by
manufactoring for me a failing grade in
Chemistry. This conspiracy obviously goes
deeper even than I thought ! I am beginning
to realize that the pre-med program was merely elaborate camoflauge, a superstructure
dangled before my eyes, to divert me from
the real pre-law, pre-banking command control
itself.

I have therefore made new plans to
infiltrate the central coordinating complex
by becoming a government and economics split
major with an emphasis on accounting and
business methods suitable for securing a
surveillance outpost for penetrating the
business and financial fields.

In order to insure my eventual success,
I have joined a final club, because I have
been getting the distinct feeling lately that
the true brains behind this whole dastardly
operation are concealed just in that area !

By the way, did I tell you about the
other night, when this other fellow and I
drank four entire bottles of bourbon together,
and we had to lie down all night in the
gutter outside the club?

Boy, did our heads ache !

With My Fondest Regards,

I remain, Yours Truly,

Your Loving Son,

a.t.

Section

3

Forbidden Fruits: The Groves Of Academe

Vanitas

Of all the obstacles put into my path by that pack of crazed paranoics out to get me and mine, exams are by far the most insidious, and now that I am beyond their stratagems I feel I can tell the whole sordid story with the lack of objectivity so necessary to slander of the first order.

It all starts a good week before the beginning of the examination period proper with the posting of the exam schedules, a healthy whiff of halitosis from the jaws of death if there ever was one. Bright and early some morning in May, I pass the ominous palimpsest on my way to lunch. I immediately go back to bed and sleep until the first day beginning with a "t". (This is an old Indian trick also used for ridding oneself of the evil eye and St. Vitus' Dance. It doesn't work.)

Arising at the crack of dusk, I confront the presumptuous papyrus with an air of quaint surprise, such as one might employ when coming suddenly upon an old schoolmaster or a dead dog. After some experience in these matters, I know that since I have only two exams, they will be on the first and last days of exam period. Consequently, I examine the listings at either end of the sheet, which comprises a good fortnight in about six yards of gothic minuscule type.

At this point, my eye catches an unusual notice: Please note that due to overcrowding some exams will be given in the Central Kitchen, Park St. Under and the University Squash Courts. It comes as no surprise that students with names from A to B will be taking the exam in a gym and everyone from Catarrh , J. to Ztumpf will be in some velvet seraglio; I'm used to that kind of thing.

It's also about this time that I discover that the exam is tomorrow morning. That's all right, though, since even though I haven't been to any of the lectures in the course, I've done none of the reading. All that remains to be done is to go over the books, which is best accomplished with a short hop or a half-skip. Sometimes I go over the books thirty or forty times. Naturally, a good night's sleep is the best preparation of all, so I go straight to bed.

The next morning, which comes about fifteen minutes later, is heralded by the massed droning of a dozen alarm clocks. I need that many because I have developed a form of karate which allows me to overpower those timepieces while still asleep; on any given morning I can get no more than three off before awakening. After a quick shower, the effectiveness of which is somewhat reduced by my taking it, due to morning grogginess, in a closet, I head for breakfast.

Upon arriving in the dining room, I realize that the room in which the exam is being given is nine kilometers from where I stand, and to suffer any chance of getting there before noon I have to skip breakfast. Needless to say, no one has ever heard of the building in question, as it lies in a part of Cambridge marked by sea-dragons and windgods on the maps.

The room, which is packed with folding tables and chairs set about a quarter of an inch from each other, is almost full when I get there. A notice on a blackboard indicates that English 144b, Literature in the Age of Boredom, should sit at tables with numbers divisible by three except those which rhyme with e'en. Biology 946 and Metallurgy 2,367a are sharing the room. I locate a place at an acceptable table, which is entirely covered with mashed applesauce and grapefruit soda. The chair is only slightly less comfortable than a mansard roof. The floor is littered with de-inflated balloons and basketballs.

I find myself completely surrounded by noisy girls. For some reason, the talk immediately before exams always involves either the Gadsden Purchase or Tennyson. In this case it is the latter, and one particularly noxious Medusa is quoting "In Memoriam" in French. The lowing of the cattle throughout the room is broken by the muzzein-like call for the beginning of the exam by the proctor. The examinations are distributed starting at the opposite end of the room, and ten minutes later I receive my copy. I take out my six felt-tipped pens, chosen for their dullness and tendency to splotch, and examine the exam.

Just as things are beginning to settle down, the proctor comes over the loudspeaker again: "Students in 144b, Question 2a should read 'gorb farx mag schlemm schnorf mixlle Newton Upper Falls.'" That is all very enlightening, and I am not surprised to discover that there is no question 2a. I make a mental note to strangle the wretch, and proceed with my preparation.

It is at this point that I notice the wallah across the table, who, to prevent cheating by people who can read Sanskrit upside down from four feet away, is in Biology 946. He is in the process of dissecting a rather large brown rat, which he has been allowed to bring into the exam room as reference material. He has just reached the intestines. At the other end of the table, a fellow in Metallurgy 2367 is operating a hydraulic slide rule and arc-welding a bit of metal to an anvil.

After answering seven of the fifty-six identification passages in something under the allotted eleven minutes, I move on to the twenty-seven essay questions. They are all of the standard type: "The natural function of literature as literature is to fulfill what Redundo de Biscuit has so aptly called 'the imperative for creative naivete of universal presumption.' Discuss, with specific reference to the peach poems of the younger Wharton."

Before too long, I have drifted off into a deep reverie in which a crowd of proctors is being called to account for crimes against humanity in administering the exams. They whimper that they were only following orders, but atrocity films of dark, overcrowded exam rooms settle their hash. I awake to the sound of the braying loudspeaker, scrawl "time" at the end of my notebook, and rush from the room.

Walking back across the river, I am overtaken by the noxious female from the exam, who sweeps by wmth her attendant Byzantines, loudly proclaiming the proper answers to every question. Judging by the high acidity and swift undertow of the Charles, they shouldn't find the bodies before Flag Day.

A HISTORY OF THE UNIVERSITY

The primeval collegians were outfitted with only crude stone-cutting tools and primitive slide carousels.

I. INTRODUCTION

When our gruff, ill-smelling ancestors assembled crude colloquia of their fellow savages before a convenient cave mouth and demonstrated to them that by the vigorous rubbing together of sticks a small spark, then a flame, and finally a blaze might be produced, they were engaging in an activity that we take quite for granted: making a fire. It was also, however, the forerunner of the process we now call education. These beginnings, to be sure, were modest by our standards. The first lecterns were rough-hewn clumps of stones. The first blackboards were nothing more than the damp and poorly illuminated walls of caves, actually gray in color. The first chalk did not exist. Initial developments were small, but they were like a funny little train with only one car. Destination? The future.

The university as we know it today, of course, was not inscribed upon the page of history until the Middle Ages. Thus were added to civilization's "general store" of progress not only the stirrup, the fetid wound, and the top-loading container, but also the college and the Pre-Professional Institute. The actual beginning, however, came long before the medieval period. The inquisitive spirit that is the basis of contemporary intellectual life is as old as many igneous rocks. The yearning for knowledge, the quest for understanding, the search for a short, comprehensible answer—all these fanned the spark that produced the flame that finally gave birth to the blaze of modern education.

II. IN OLDEN TIMES

The shamanistic instruction rites of primitive cultures are among the earliest predecessors of modern educational institutions. The lengthy, and occasionally bloody, rituals served to pass along important tribal history and social information to primitive boys whose brains were smaller than your fist; courses included The Vexing of Disagreeable Neighboring Tribesmen, Principles of Subsistence Agriculture, and The Theory and Application of Spirit-Inhabited Vegetation.

In the most primitive hunting and foraging societies, education was at first a simple matter based upon semesters lasting only one or two days. Ironically, today's farsighted experts predict that some day in the misty, utopian future, educational institutions will function on a similar basis. Before the middle of the twenty-first century, they say, the average citizen in the United World Federation will be able to master his finite, highly specialized cultural function in a matter of hours. Unpaid machines will do the rest.

III. THE CLASSICAL WORLD OF LONG AGO

Socrates: Now then, do you agree that the men of Achaea share in the parts of virtue so that some have one and some another, but that this man they call Socrates "the gadfly" possesses all virtue and always will?

Socrates: Yes, Socrates, certainly. Very true.

Socrates: And that, according to our agreement, to contradict this man Socrates is neither just nor temperate, wise nor advisable?

Socrates: Yes, I am inclined to agree.

Socrates: Good. You may administer my spanking.

This fragment from Plato's timeless *Meno* expresses a conception of pedagogy as a volatile contact between two minds, a dramatic exchange between conflicting personalities. It should help one appreciate the immeasurable gains made by the ancient Greeks since those ruder days when society judged its learned ones by how high they could count.

What actions angered the gods? Which ones made them sleepy? What was "right conduct"? And who was this funny little man, Man, anyhow? These inquiries consumed the curious Greeks—and gave their parents some headaches, too!

IV. HISTORY'S FIRST SEMESTER

Prehistoric proto-semesters were first geared to the female menstrual cycle, a little-understood phenomenon to which early man attached enormous mystical significance. Teaching sessions in one tribe lasted, according to a fragmentary and dubious record, through "three courses of the she-wound." More primitive tribes determined the duration of learning rites on no more sound a basis than the attention spans of the students: "When the young men no longer make marks on their clay tablets, then is the time to test them and let them go home."

The astrologers of the remarkable Mayan civilization of South America performed ingenious celestial calculations centuries before the birth of Christ and estimated with astonishing precision the length of the true, or solar, semester. As a result, the Mayan educational system was one of the most efficient the world has ever known. Examination dates were fixed according to an elaborate astrological chart of galactic events, and lectures always began on time. Classes ended ten days before the winter festival of the sun god, leaving ample time for students to secure travel arrangements and acquire stone cheeses for family members and close friends.

The old Julian system of computing semesters did not account for registration or orientation periods; by the 1360s, the system had become so distorted that final examinations were given during Parents' Week. During the enthusiastic nationalism of the French Revolution, a brief attempt was made to make semesters coincide exactly with the solar year by pretending there was no summer. This quickly proved unworkable.

Interesting recent studies in biorhythms have found that if a student is placed in a cave with only artificial light, he will naturally adopt a system of two semesters of 13 weeks each, with a month-long minisession after Christmas.

V.   IN THE DAYS OF YORE

Although genuine universities did not arise until well into the eleventh century, the first sophomores appeared considerably earlier. Isolated specimens of freshmen date back to pre-Christian times, when hapless "firsters," as they were known, were employed as "beast-bait" in the procurement of wild animals for public recreations. Vesuvius' lava flow preserved for all eternity one Pompeii freshman in the act of trying to talk his way out of a foreign language requirement. The feverish grimace on the young boy's face raises goose pimples on the spines of visitors to that historic site even today.

In the late tenth century, nomadic hordes of bloodthirsty upperclassmen swept down from the Pyrenees in Northern Italy and terrorized peaceful lowland settlements of first-year students. The older scholars emerged victorious from the heated ten-year confrontation that followed, instituting the barbarous practice of "hazing" their defenseless captives. In one particularly gruesome incident, a gangly youngster wearing only a tonsurelike beanie was forced to stand on a mead-hall table and translate Arabic commentaries on Aristotle.

Hazing briefly rose to intolerable levels in the thirteenth century, inciting sporadic rioting in Bologna and Ferrara around 1255. Skirmishes continued throughout the remainder of the century, and it was not until Marco Polo opened up the Eastern drug trade in 1295 that upperclassmen became noticeably more mature and considerate about the whole matter.

Medieval schoolboys were forced to attend their classes in the rubble of war-torn cathedrals.

VI.   THE ANCIENT, ORIGINAL LIBRARY

Kindly Saint Benedict unwittingly spawned a fad which was quick to become an enduring craze: that of the library and, indirectly, the library card. In his Rule, he "strongly" recommended that a collection of books and educational reprints be centrally located within each self-governing monastery so that the monks might "learn humility from, and take joy in, laboriously translating the works of the Four Fathers in airless rooms, by candlelight, with quill pens, empty stomachs, and ink made from the urine of sheep. Perhaps this will also take their minds off the babes." [Latin *pudenda*].

The Harvard Lampoon
Big Book of College Life

76

Benedict's Rule also suggested that monastic printing presses should be abolished, since these led to frivolous thinking and had not yet been invented. As a result, the monasteries were forced to "farm out" work, whence arose monastic schools. There, illiterate peasant boys were given the most tedious and least scatological of the copying and translation material as assignments. Benedictine teachers decided to allow the students to finish them at home. Since the boys had been so long away, however, many of them found on their return that their parents had died, their siblings had grown up and moved away and the homes themselves had been razed by barbarian armies. There was nothing to do but provide homes for such students—the first recorded use of dormitories—and to seize their lands in lieu of tuition, room and board payments. In return, the boys were given more difficult assignments and, later, permission to translate thier own diplomas onto parchment.

VII. AN INTERESTING NOTE

Citizens of the Western World are often surprised to discover that not all societies hold education in such high esteem. Formal schooling does not exist, for example, among the big cats, nor, indeed, among any animals other than man.

Hard to believe? Even some human societies confer low status upon the educated. Consider the treatment given Western-educated natives of Mali when they return to their homeland. Upon the arrival of one of these upwardly mobile globetrotters, Mali villagers abruptly drop discussion of their complicated mythic cosmology and belabor the newcomer with tedious discussion of rainfall and dead relatives. These shrewd folk then point with childish wonder at the man's wristwatch, attempt to rub "charisma" off his clothing and ask goggle-eyed questions about the White Savior God. After several days of such mock deference, the villagers kill and eat their native son, using his hardback boots for roofing material.

The educational practices of other hunter-gatherer societies lend credence to the claim that our primitive forebears may have seen education as punishment to be inflicted upon those unfit for hunting or warfare. One North Kenyan myth describes tiny men with inordinately large heads performing a "degradation ritual" after four harvest years' exemption from physical labor. These students— or "grandmothers," as they are referred to in the myth—must don filthy skirts, such as only the most decrepit widows in the tribe wear, and then smear their faces with ash. Their stomachs are bound with twine, and in their noses they carry large oblong lumps of old sago pancakes, the stale orts of a long-finished meal. These disgustingly costumed grandmothers hobble about the community after their graduation, seeking any odd jobs that the other members of the tribe might deign to give them. The ceremony, of course, has its greatest appeal for children, who greet the ghostlike miscreants with shrieks of laughter or mock fear.

Brutal initiation rites dominated a young scholar's college years during the nineteenth century. These practices were later slightly modified.

The Groves of Academe

VIII. ENGLAND'S BONNY PAST

The poet Geoffrey Chaucer annoyed the intellectuals of fourteenth-century England by using the proceeds from his famous *Canterbury Tales* to purchase gaudy articles of clothing that were actually cruel parodies of accepted academic garb. He would dress up in his outrageous costumes, inhale pints of frothy beer through the nostrils of his upturned nose and proclaim in his loudest voice: "Lerne ye to wryte at hame, in they speer tame."

Although the British Museum owns several illuminated manuscripts of medieval course listings, or *menus*, the college brochure as such did not really come into its own until Gutenberg printed "This is Gottingen College" in 1458. Indeed, Luther pronounced college brochures anathema shortly thereafter and they were forced underground in Germany until Napoleon's invasion brought his blanket "Edict for the Emancipation and Legalization of Prussian College-Related Materials."

Less traditional classroom settings such as this open-air poetry seminar taught by inner-city youths became popular during the 1960's.

IX. VISTAS OF EDUCATION

The overworked young scholars of this country might be pleased to learn that the education of their Indian counterparts is a long process of forgetting! Perhaps this accounts for the thousands of pilgrimages to India made yearly by failing students from Cal Poly. In any event, the exercises for achievement of *barbo thol*, or "paralysis of the intellect," developed over the millennia by Oriental sages, differ significantly from the ones practiced at American junior colleges since World War II.

At the Sangha for Six-Pointed Space—a rural experimental school near Delhi, roughly equivalent to our own Hampshire College—students begin with the patient unlearning of axioms, theories and paradigms that relate these facts into a meaningful whole, and finally advance to the deterioration of all verbal and numerical skills ("Sophomore Standing"). Having achieved a modicum of self-discipline and personal autonomy—often through a year's leave of absence from the sangha—the mature student then sets about to master the atrophy of all physical sensation, the annihilation of memory and the loss of all intuition of time, space, substance and causality. At this point he is prepared to graduate and assume his responsible role in a society of free citizens.

Graduation Week for the young Indian races by in a dizzying round of parties and dances, ceremonial speeches and heartfelt farewells to friends. The climax comes when the seniors doff their mortarboards in unison and dissolve in a radiant sphere of Immortal Light. This ceremony—one of great significance for the parents in attendance—is followed by another longer one for degree candidates who have not managed to meet their requirements. Each of these students is conducted to the podium, where he is tortured for all eternity by the goddess Indrani, a dog-headed deity bearing a noose of entrails in her hands.

CONCLUSION:

Whither the Western university in the wearying years ahead? Will it weather the winds of the waning wealth of man, or wither in the welter of the whimsical human will? Whichever, whatever: with luck it will withstand the wilting waters of wayward wisdom and of wit. What ho! Thank you very much.

In the future, universities will probably look like this.

HOW TO WRITE A 5-PAGE PAPER

1. In writing the traditional five-page paper, always repeat the title in your first sentence.

2. Triple space and use genenerous margins. (For the traditional six-or seven-page paper, quadruple-space and use even more generous margins.)

3. Always turn in your papers late to assure special attention, even in large, overcrowded lecture courses.

4. Tell them what you are going to say, say it, say it again, say it maybe one more time, then tell them that you said it.

5. Always repeat yourself.

6. When preparing your manuscript, you can safely skip a page number somewhere in the middle of the paper, since instructors only look at the last page number when gauging its length. (Note the smooth transition in the example from page two to page four.)

7. Always spell out numbers.

8. Include an impressive footnote.

9. Don't be afraid to reiterate.

10. If a word at the end of a line is a short one, you can repeat it at the beginning of the next line, because the eye of the reader generally skips over it (see example, page one, lines nine and ten).

11. Define words.

12. Always equivocate; qualify where possible.

13. Use polysyllabic words and at least one foreign term.

14. Remember: redundancy, redundancy, redundancy.

<u>The Conceptions of Freedom in Kate Chopin's</u>

<u>The Awakening and the Ones in Mark Twain's</u>

<u>Huckleberry Finn: Where They Differ and</u>

<u>How Come</u>

D. Arnold Swansong

English **101**

Late

One must first note the
quite extraordinary handling
of the concept of freedom in "Kate"
Chopin (pronounced Show - pan)'s
The Awakening and Mark Twain's
(really named Samuel Clemens, but
he named his "pen name" after a
word for how deep the river was-
the Mississippi River, which is the
the longest river in the world if
you count its tributaries, which
include the Ohio, the Missouri
and the Ouachita- when a steamboat
was on it) handling of the same
concept in his book Huckleberry

Finn.

The Grosset Webster Dictionary
(New Revised Edition, 1966, Grosset and
Dunlap, New York, page two hundred
forty-six) defines "freedom" as
"1. Exemption from power or control
by another; liberty; independence.
2. Frankness; openness. 3. Liberal-
ity. 4. Special privilege; immunity.
5. Exemption from necessity. 6. Facility; ease. 7. License; violation of
rules of decorum. 8. A free, uncondit-
ional grant." I think that it should be
clear to anyone who has made more than a
cursory examination of these books that
what we are dealing with is mostly
definition one with a little bit of

definition four and perhaps even a
little bit of definition seven. It
would seem that having divided the
subject into these primary areas for
discussion we can now examine it more
closely to ascertain the distinctions,
contrasts, differences and disparities
between the two literary works.
One could safely assert that Chopin's
book or novel seems most likely to deal
more with definition one; whereas it seems
to me at least that Twain's book or novel
leans in its intention more toward
definition seven.

    As we have seen, there are indeed
major differences in the conception of freedom as they are portrayed in Kate Chopin's

The Awakening and in Mark Twain's bildungs-
roman (German for "novel of education") about
a young American boy growing up, which we know
as Huckleberry Finn.

BIBLIOGRAPHY

Bartholow V. Crawford, <u>American Literature College</u>
<u>Outline Series</u> (New York 1953)

<u>Das Deutsches Worterbuch: Moderne Amerikanisch</u>
<u>Englische Gegenwartssprache</u> (Chicago, 1966)

<u>The Grosset Webster Dictionary</u> (New York, 1966)

Frank N. Magill, ed. <u>Masterpieces of World</u>
<u>Literature in Digest Form</u> (New York, 1949)

"Mississippi River", <u>The Columbia Viking Desk</u>
<u>Encyclopedia</u> (New York, 1953), pp. 663-664

THE CHANCES ARE THAT YOU HAVEN'T FOUND MUCH OF THIS ISSUE TO BE VERY FUNNY

AND NOW YOU'VE TURNED TO THIS PAGE HOPING TO READ A JOKE, AND INSTEAD YOU SEE A PICTURE OF A HARVARD PROFESSOR!

WELL, DON'T BE ALARMED!! WE PROFESSORS ARE HUMOROUS FELLOWS. IN FACT, WE TEND TO BE FUNNIER THAN THE AVERAGE JOE!

SUPPOSE YOU WERE WALKING DOWN THE STREET AND SAW A PEER OF YOURS ON TOP OF A BALL WITH SMOKE COMING OUT OF HIS EARS. WOULD YOU LAUGH? NO.

NOW IMAGINE YOU SAW A FAMOUS HARVARD PROFESSOR, LIKE JAMES Q. WILSON, ON TOP OF A BALL. WOULD YOU LAUGH? OF COURSE!

DISTINGUISHED PROFESSORS CAN GET THEIR STUDENTS TO LAUGH AT ANYTHING! WATCH ME CRACK UP THIS GROUP WITH AN INCREDIBLY CRETINOUS QUIP!

WASN'T THAT EASY? A JOKE LIKE THAT WORKS EVERY TIME FOR A PROFESSOR~ AND MAKES US POPULAR WITH THE KIDS!

IN THE GAME OF HUMOR, THE PLAYERS ARE MORE IMPORTANT THAN THE CONTENT!

A CHILD MAKING NOISES WITH HIS ARMPIT AT THE DINNER TABLE IS NOT FUNNY

BUT A MINISTER MAKING THOSE SAME SOUNDS DURING A SERVICE IS A LAUGH RIOT!

A PLUMBER WHO WEARS A LIGHT-UP BOW TIE TO WORK IS CONSIDERED A RETARD.

A NOBEL PRIZE BIOLOGIST WHO WEARS ONE TO A COCKTAIL PARTY BECOMES A COMIC GENIUS!

WELL KIDS, THANKS FOR THIS REAL DEEP RAP SESSION...

BUT I'M LATE FOR MY LECTURE!

"NANCY AND NIHILISM"

Ernie Bushmiller is perhaps the most misunderstood writer of our times. Denigrated as the base voluptuary, feared as the angry social anarchist, dismissed as the degenerate pseudo-prophet, Ernie Bushmiller, the man, has long blocked the path to rational, critical consideration of his art and of his mythic (dare we deny it?) character, Nancy. Why another lecture on Ernie Bushmiller? In this lecture I hope to divorce for the first time the man from his work, examining the art first on its own merits and only afterward taking potshots at the man himself.

Let us hasten to the extant texts. I believe the basic format of Bushmiller's thought during his Middle Period is best encapsulated in the much-discussed "gumdrop incident" of the early 1950s. As you will recall, the first frame shows Nancy before a gumdrop machine, labeled "GUMDROPS," wishing that she might have one. The penultimate frame reveals a construction worker entering upon this scene, not far beyond the machine. In the final frame, the worker is operating a pneumatic drill, and the machine, rattled by the drill's vibrations, is pouring out gumdrop after gumdrop; in boldface letters Nancy remarks, "Wow." What does it mean? Who has granted Nancy's prayer? Professor Bacon, adopting Bergson's approach and asking, "Why do we laugh?" concludes that we laugh because it is "funny," and because it offers us a release for the laughter pent up within us. But such a view has been conclusively refuted by T. S. Eliot, who points out, "But it's not funny, and we don't laugh." It is the lack or privation of humor that Northrop Frye alludes to in his observation "There are two basic narrative movements in Bushmiller—a movement sideways and a movement further sideways."

Perhaps this may be better seen in the more expanded format of a Sunday strip, for which I think the recent "Bandana-Banana substitution" will serve us well. Here Nancy, conversing with a younger child, points out, in an unusually outspoken political digression, "Prices are really going up these days." In the next frame, her companion agrees, observing, "Yes, especially for food. They're selling bananas for $1.00 each." Nancy, skeptical, challenges: $1.00 each! Show me." In the final frame the puzzle is unraveled, for there are three bandanas hanging in a storefront window with a sign saying, "BANDANAS, $1.00 EACH." Nancy quips, "That doesn't say bananas, it says *bandanas.*" The similarities between this strip and the above daily strip of several years earlier are striking. Most superficially, we observe that neither is funny. But "Hark, little lower layer." Why are Nancy's remarks always unnecessary? And this is just the point. Professor Porte is on the right track when he writes of the passage:

> Do you see? The joke is being played on Nancy herself and it is a cruel one at that. Nancy is so timid or suppressed that she can utter nothing witty. We don't laugh, because we don't "get it." But in a dual sense, neither does Nancy "get it."
>
> Her surrogate mother, Aunt Fritzie, due to an inexplicably absent husband, does not get it either. And while Aunt Fritzie's conservative dress and exposed shin do not conclusively point to a latent lesbianism, neither can the reader confidently dismiss such an inference. Moreover, Nancy's Trinity is shown to consist of three phallic bananas (which magically replace the seemingly innocuous bandanas), while the providential figure of the "gumdrop incident," the workman's vibrating pneumatic drill, seen in this light, admits of no ambiguity.

It may be helpful at this juncture to digress briefly in order that we may examine the Bushmiller journal before tackling one of the so-called problem strips. Amid the frenetic scribblings that Bushmiller failed to burn during his Crazy Period, we have the following fragment, apparently referring to the Sunday strip just discussed:

Grass—green
Sky—blue
Clouds—white(?)
$1.00—$3.00 each?

Fascinating as these notes are in their revelation of Bushmiller in the agonizing throes of the creative movement, they can only hint at the greater treasures lost forever, burned by an artist tortured by self-doubt and coerced by embarrassed relatives.

On February 3, 1973, a biframe Nancy cartoon came out that rocked the comic strip world. It went like this:

Frame one: Sluggo, mouth open, three beads of sweat flying into the air, is viewing three fish floating in midair over a table and asks, "Am I losing my mind?" In the same frame Nancy answers, "No."

Frame two: Sluggo, *sans* beads of sweat, yet mouth open, continues to watch the three fish as Nancy explains, "My new fishbowl is made of invisible glass."

Nancy's reply, of course, makes no sense and yet, although flawed, I think the strip works. Far from being aberrant, the strip is the most radically twentieth-century work in the Bushmiller corpus.

So we have come full circle. Yet Bushmiller cannot blithely pyrne in Yeats' gyre, nor can he bounce up Eliot's staircase; he cannot even drown in Charybdis' vortex. Rather, he is doomed to a fate worse still. He must endlessly shuffle back and forth like Sisyphus without the hill, like a graduate student without a fellowship, like Goethe without the umlaut. Such is the horrifying annihilation of Bushmiller's vision.

FACULTY OF ARTS AND SCIENCES

COURSES OF INSTRUCTION
1978-79

OFFICIAL REGISTER OF
HARVARD UNIVERSITY

Afro-American Studies 1: **Unthreatening Black Literature.**
A. B. Carter.
Readings conforming to the standards of white liberal educators, including *Native Son, Go Tell It on the Mountain, Raisin in the Sun* and *Invisible Man.*
Note: For beginning Negroes only.
Full course. Hours to be arranged.

Afro-American Studies 100: **The Magnificence of Blackness.**
Visiting Adjunct Assistant Lecturer.
Examines the grace, splendor, beauty, nobility, majesty, elegance and grandeur of Blackness. Special attention is called to its sublimity.
Half course. (Fall term) T/Th at 2.

Anthropology 398: **Modern Studies in Anthropology.**
Erik Potter.
Effects of diminishing number of untouched primitive tribal groups on the morale of ever-expanding population of anthropological researchers; recovery of re-publishable material from the recently published past; construction of useful housewares and accessories from ancient pottery fragments.
Full course. M/W/F at 10.

Biology 255: **Appearing Brilliant.**
Members of the Staff.
Nobel laureates will discuss topics remote from their tiny areas of expertise. Students will be expected to observe the physical gestures and grooming attending narrow brilliance, including meditative eye squinting, pensive upward gazes, disheveled longish hair, neat but casual dress, digressions implying liberal political sympathies and use of Yiddishisms by Gentile professors.
Half course. (Fall term) M/W at 11.

English 250: **Bad Verse.**
Peter Haas and Staff.
Authors for study include Malory, Lydgate, Skelton, Spenser, Campion, Jonson, Herrick, Carew, Prior, Gray, Collins, Cowper, Wordsworth, Landor, Emerson, Tennyson, Arnold, Pater, Dickinson, Hardy and Robert Penn Warren.
Prerequisite: Some knowledge of bad prose.
Half course. (Spring term) T/Th at 2.

English 289: **The Silent Jury.**
Janet McClaughlin.
House plants in the novels of Jane Austen.
Note: Primarily for graduate students.
Half course. (Spring term) W 2–5.

English 300: **Major Themes That Can't Miss.**
Heather Sorenson.
Themes so all-encompassing that they cannot possibly
be unrelated to any given work of fiction. Motifs to be
dealt with include appearance vs. reality, alienation and
discovery, good vs. evil, nature vs. art, and the journey.
Full course. T/Th at 11.

Geology 10. **Dirt.**
Nathaniel Landau.
Where found; what to do about.
Half course. (Spring term) T/Th/(S) at 9.

Government 155: **Upward Mobility Techniques.**
Terence Sorel.
A survey of the major modes of obsequious self-
degradation, including kowtowing, buttering-up, apple-
polishing, ass-licking, brown-nosing, and butt-sucking.
Special attention given to the techniques of asking
pertinent questions and reading the professor's latest
article.
Prerequisite: Some experience on high school honor
rolls.
Half course. (Spring term) M/W at 10, with optional
sections for those really interested.

Government 174: **Decision-making.**
William Weisburg.
Course will most likely deal with theories of solving
problems devoid of content. Maybe we'll do policies
studies and/or process methodologies; we can't really
know for sure until the course is under way. Any other
vacuous abstractions of special interest to students may
merit discussion.
Full course. Hours to be arranged at a conference to be
set up at a time to be agreed upon; contact Professor
Weisburg.

Philosophy 340: **Wittgenstein.**
Harvey D. Lichtblau.
Talk, books, learn, prove, there.
Half course. (Spring term) W 11-11:05.

Cliff Notes for the Total Novel

NOTE: Remember that no mere outline can provide interminable joys of countless hours hunched over a book while the parade passes you by; but if you think this lousy trot is going to put enough polish on your literary act to get you even near that peasant-bloused poetess with the rude muchachas in your English section, you might as well bag it now: take a powder on over to the Ale House and get back with the muscle boys where you belong.

PILOT OUTLINE
CHAPTER ONE

SUMMARY: The first chapter deals with the opening themes of the book; that is, those treated in the first several pages. We are immediately made to understand that the hero is in fact the hero of the book itself. The hero does not know that he is a hero, or even that he is in the story at all. Significantly, he thinks he is a real guy, and not even in a book. We are brought into the thick of the action by the swift turning of pages and by the way in which our eye seems to skim over entire passages and words we don't know as we draw nearer to completing our assignment.

COMMENT: A Structural Analysis. This opening chapter deserves close attention. In it the author uses a number of techniques which he will employ again and again throughout the story. The author will often use "words" to communicate his most private and profound "ideas." He will often place these "words" into "sentences" and use the technique of arranging these sentences into "paragraphs" to make his meaning clear.

CHAPTER TWENTY-SEVEN

Yes, foambrain, this is the last chapter of the book. Always skip right to the end after you have checked out the beginning. Who knows if you'll have time to read now that practice has started, so at least you'll know how it turns out. The work as a whole concludes with an extended metaphor of life, a lot of drippy garbage just like you've got on all the posters in your room. The sentences start to run on and on, the punctuation stops completely, and if you can read three words straight without having to look them up, you don't need this trot, you snotty little grind.

CHAPTER TWO

If you're really out to butt-suck this term, this chapter is worth a look. Here the structural tension apparent in the work becomes apparent and is heightened as we begin to contrast the endless lines of dense, dark words with the airy, white void of the margins of the book is brought home by the librarian, who tries to hit us for three bucks for keeping our fictive world out three hours late on reserve. We do not understand, and dramatic conflict is brought into the story as we pick the little wonk up by the collar and hold him high above the plane of ordinary reality, until he allows us to transcend the classical unities of space and time and keep the private vision of the author at home with us as long as we goddam please.

COMMENT: In marked contrast to Chapter One, Chapter Two comes considerably later in the book. In this chapter we become familiar with the mind of the hero, through the representation of "thoughts." In much the same way, just as we reach the last page, the chapter seemingly ends. This prepares us for the next chapter, which almost without warning begins on the following page.

CHAPTER THREE

SUMMARY: In this chapter, the author starts playing games and giving us the runaround, the way his type always does. He doesn't even bother with capital letters anymore, or people, or nothing, he just goes ahead la-de-da with a lot of "stream of consciousness;" ... to hell with this guy.

COMMENT: Bring the book back to the library, where it belongs, and give these notes back to the oxhead you stole them from. Skip this stuff and start making some yardage wtih that really built section leader of yours instead. Wear a scarf, be cool, and put some real points up on that scoreboard. Tackle those big art-type subjects with kick-ass metaphors and power smiles so intense and bristling with significance, you'll be halfway there in no time. If you're as smooth as I think you are, you'll have the course aced by morning. Way to go, meatloaf.

"RELATIVITY SPEAKING"

One of the sillier myths of the Post-*Sputnik* Era is that ordinary people can't understand the theory of relativity. From a scientific standpoint, it's hard to imagine how this got started, let alone where it began. In fact, like the work of all truly great thinkers, Einstein's logical masterpiece may be explained with a few analogies drawn from your own kitchen or workbench.

Just think about this: what makes bits of household dirt fly into the family vacuum cleaner? Gravity, you'd say, and right you'd be. A sidilar force is the motor that keeps our universe running smoothly. As you might expect, though, on this larger scale there are some extra nettlesome problems.

Einstein thought so, too. He noticed that at every wedding he had ever attended, the beak and wings of the swan sculpted in ice had melted before the body. The Newtonian (wrong) theory of gravity could not account for this. All ice was supposed to melt at the same rate. In a moment of inspiration, Einstein realized that melting was uniform throughout the attractive frozen centerpieces — but time wasn't!

He had hit upon what he called the "hard part" of relativity. Einstein saw that an inverted fish tank set over the beak or wings of the swan would contain only a little ice and a lot of air (actually, nothing), while there was a great deal more ice in the bird's torso. This additional mass in the same volume would lead to a greater gravitational force. In this case, it was strong enough to bend light. (Light happens to be the lightest thing we know of, although the words are etymologically different.) Einstein gave superdense objects like ice sculptures the name "prisms."

The key to this brain teaser is in one's point of view. Take a journey of the mind into the unimaginably dense heart of the frozen swan. Once you are acclimatized to the chill, you see that all the ice molecules really are turning into water molecules at the normal rate. However, there are so very, very many of them (think of the ants you can see from a skyscraper and you'll have a rough idea of the number, if you multiply by one *hundred*!), each of them tugging insistently at the light trying to escape, that it may be several minutes before the outside observer can detect what is "business as usual" for you. In effect, time has been bent. If this is a little hard for you to grasp, watch the sky around Uranus for a few nights. It's the same principle.

Einstein's theory has significance for more than caterers' goods, planets and so on. It determines the whole order of our universe, even its shape — though many Soviet scientists privately disagree. It is now definitely known that the universe is constantly expanding, much like the rings of a sequoia tree (on display in most California state parks). We can't discuss this point in detail here, but a simple proof is in the fact that airplanes, subject to space-time interplay, get bigger — and noisier! — every year. Density is the *limiting factor* in this expansion, a kind of cosmic traffic signal. If the universe is superdense (red light) it will always have the roughly spherical shape of the ice swan's body, and will someday collapse back on itself, just as the swan will begin to shrink (not really, of course). A somewhat lower density (yellow light) will allow the universe to keep on expanding, in the shape of a water puddle without an edge, until it stops. The lowest density of all (go-ahead signal) would give the universe the form of an endlessly expanding saddle or swaybacked cheese grater. This modified grater shape is called a "pseudosphere" by scientists, since it in no way resembles a sphere.

Contrary to popular opinion, Einstein frequently had to say, "I just don't know." Aside from the density of the universe, many of relativity's effects remain the stuff of speculative fiction — probably a good thing for all of us. For instance, no one has yet shown what would happen (try it yourself and you'll see why) if one of two identical pieces of rock candy (in experiments, frequently substituted for ice swans because of the latter's volatility) were placed on a windowsill and the other accelerated through space at nine tenths of the speed of light. Most physicists think that the second confection would not notice any change, while the other would grow old and hardly recognize its twin when it returned. (The experiment would have to be performed with rock candy first to make sure it was safe for humans.) In agriculture, we may still find that last year's freeze of the Florida citrus crop was a needless disaster. One thing is certain — we can be glad that the charming Fraulein Berger kept Einstein waiting those crucial twenty minutes.

THE NUTTY PROFESSOR
OR KIDS DIE THE DARNDEST DEATHS

STUDY
THE BEST MEDICINE

Every college student must one day ask, "Gee, how am I going to pass my courses?" Nine times out of ten the answer is: Study! Nobody but a real "brain" gets away without studying, and only in fairy tales even then. The average Joe or Josie (i.e., *you*) must spend a good part of every day in study or else be content to "eat the dust" of more successful and popular scholars.

In general terms, study is aimed at the learning of "subject matter." That phrase puts its finger on the nutshell: your course material is the subject, and you are the sovereign. No book will ever read you, no problem set will ever tear you up in a rage of frustration. This is as it should be, and with this thought in mind you may decide whether you wish to reign or to rule. Most balanced minds eventually choose the latter option. If for some reason you do not, just slap down our helping hands right now. Don't waste any more of your time or ours. No hard feelings — it's your funeral. Of course, if you do keep reading, we promise to like you.

Even from down here on the page the look of healthy determination is visible on the faces of you who have chosen to persevere. For those who have set their eyes upon the spinning grindstone, the most important part of the task has been completed. All that remains is to digest a few helpful hints. *Bon appetit*!

1. *Read, read, read.* Whether he knows it or not, anyone who has ever stared at the back of a box of Cocoa Puffs has been reading. Millions of people use the scholar's "magic wand" every day without realizing the tremendous power they possess. It lies at hand for any clever, ambitious, conscientious young person to grasp. Use it — but use it wisely.

   a. *Find out your assignments.* If only you'll do a little investigating, you will discover that most teachers make a point of telling you what they expect you to read. Naturally, they do it in their own academic Morse code. Frequently examination of apparently meaningless blackboard handwriting displays and mimeo typography samples will reveal names and even authors of books that the instructor, whether consciously or not, would like you to read.

   b. *Read your assignments.* Don't try to second-guess your teacher. Even the best student-constructed reading list will only set an instructor off in a fit of pique. Teachers are dangerous when crossed. The story of the smart-aleck English major who substituted *Ball Four* for *Catcher in the Rye* is all too well known.

   c. *Remember your assignments.* Of course, a book can be man's best friend. However, like any pet it can also turn into a snarling, vicious brute. A book and its pals owe you nothing. An hour after you put them down, they have forgotten all about you and are not particularly anxious to renew the acquaintance. The burden of the relationship, like it or not, is on you. If you want one of the nasty curs with you in the examination room, you'll have to drag it there, kicking and screaming, on your own mental leash. This is best accomplished by...

2. *Notes, notes, notes.* For centuries, reading and writing have gone hand in hand for the "smart set." Today, students incapable of taking a note could hardly hope to write out a whole exam, let alone produce an attractive party invitation. Certainly you could try to take notes without writing, but even inexpensive potato-block printing is a victim of pernicious stagflation and changing fashion. Furthermore, when finals time rolls around, the proctors will probably frown on your hauling a forty-pound sack of Idaho spuds into the examination room. No,

writing is here to stay as America's favorite form of impromptu literary expression. Try to get on top of the fad that promises to become a tradition.

a. *Note what you read.* Stationary letters and words are sitting ducks for the beginning writer. They are totally helpless when the enterprising novice is really bent on transferring them into his notebook. This last item is important. The over eager student who copied *Elements of Biochemistry* into *The Mill on the Floss* merely ruined two ordinarily entertaining books. Always use a notebook. If you honestly cannot, don't take to the vindictive vandalism and monstrous misuse of the usually cheerful yellow Magic Marker. So many frustrated young ruffians try the lame excuse that they "own" their books and can do anything they please with them. They also shoot horses, don't they?

b. *Note what you hear.* The old maxim might well be "Those who can't do, talk." The nonstop gabfests your instructors indulge in can be mines of information. Don't be ashamed to write while the teacher speaks; odds are he or she will be flattered as long as you've asked permission beforehand. On weekends, practice by transcribing television programs, or get a friend to read to you over the telephone. Soon you'll not only be a better student, but you'll also be able to finish other people's sentences for them. Education has many such dividends.

c. *Note what you think.* After months of devoted study, you may find your free time encumbered by nagging thoughts, conclusions and intellectual constructs. Turn this minor nuisance into a major resource by writing out these unbidden mental guests. Keep a small pastel-colored (for women) or morocco-bound (for men) diary full of such cerebral debris, and you'll find that your friends will credit you with a full emotional life at half the cost.

3. *Other general pointers*
a. Make an effort to attend classes at their scheduled times.
b. Always carry a stapler. (Not a Tot 50.)
c. Take a warm (not hot) shower before studying.
d. When there is a difficulty, make an outline.
e. Sleep soundly, but sanely.

"HUMORIZATION AND TRI-LEVEL JOKE FORMATION IN PAN TROGLODYTES"

Lecture

3

Man distinguishes himself from the other subjects in the animal kingdom by his ability to laugh and make others laugh. Or does he? Recent experimentation in the field of primate linguistics lends support to the undeniably radical view that sub-human animals may be capable of conceiving and communicating "jokes."

It is well known that lucky scientists at major research institutions around the world have achieved astonishing successes in regent years in applied in-cage study programs aimed at teaching higher non-human primates to "talk."

My assistants and I raised a sexually differentiated pair of chimpanzees (pan troglodytes) from birth in a laboratory. Our investigation proceeded along standard linguistical patternologies during the first two years and six months after the birth of the chimpanzees. The male (Leonard) and the female (Martha) acquired vocabularies at or near the 200-word level. However, at this time an alarming development occurred. At the end of a long afternoon of training procedure and vocabulary development exercises, Leonard referred to his human instructor as the equivalent of a "horse's ass." The actual construct within the computerized vocabulary program was as follows: "friend-man / is windhole / of barn dog. Want cookie." We dismissed the utterance as coincidence until the next day, when Leonard was observed to communicate the following message to Martha: "Want Martha / give Leonard lap candy. Hubba hubba." Martha appeared not to understand the communication, but after some extended prodding by Leonard, made signs indicating the following reply: "Give Martha / Etch-a-Sketch. Then eat."

In our astonishment we consulted available literature and came upon the following account in *Psychology Today*: A researcher who had raised a chimpanzee in his home from birth returned home from the university one day to discover a conspicuous mound of chimpanzee fecal material soaking into the pile of his living room rug. He asked the chimp in sign language if he were responsible for the mess, whereupon the chimp, again in sign language, indicated that the cat was the guilty party. The researcher objected, pointing out that cat droppings were never so massive as those now interacting wmth the rug. The chimp replied that he now remembered a man whom he had never seen before, wearing ragged clothes and carrying a cardboard suitcase, had entered the house before noon and squatted on the carpet. Again the researcher objected. At this point the chimp broke down and confessed, entering into a three-day guilt/embarrassment complex, throughout which the chimp refused to speak to anyone but took every opportunity to abuse the cat physically.

Our conclusion was inescapable: if chimpanzees could lie and be obscene, might they not also be able to tell jokes?

We began our secondary research. The chimpanzees' vocabularies were augmented over a one-year period with such word units as "wife," "hippie," "bippie," "sidekick" and "Adirondacks." Tertiary attention was paid to conceptual reinforcement of such structured and unstructured communicatory models as "timing," "banter" and "pace." Continued efforts were made in the attempt to overcome the chimpanzee's instinctual fear of applause and belly laughter. Significant, quantifiable results were virtually immediate.

Leonard achieved the first success. After several hours of intensive instruction, he slumped onto a stool, lit a cigar and made signs to indicate the following message: "Leonard fly from coast / arms tired." Martha rejoined with: "Martha room so little / go hall change mind." And then Leonard: "Martha nose big / smoke shower." And after a pause: "White-coat not laugh / not punish Leonard / Leonard read word card / punish word maker."

Several days later Leonard woke his instructor several hours earlier than usual and had this to say: "Leonard funny / put in barrel / baboon come to jungle / sleep tree by Leonard tree / baboon stay / neighborhood go / Take Martha / please. Ha ha ha."

Potentialities for similar research are virtually parameterless. Scientific opinion now holds that Kirlian photography is a "joke" and that the photographic vegetable aura may be nothing more astonishing than a sick attempt at humor perpetrated by insensitive chlorophyll-producing life forms. B. Reynolds Flores, Professor of Applied Thought at Stanford University, claims to have evidence that the grass in one man's lawn will "laugh" when the yard next door is mowed. Certain ores and minerals such as iron pyrite and strontium 90 have long been known to be capable of joke formation on a primitive level. If the study of primate humorization is to be advanced, as indeed it must be, then the burden is in your hands.

alm

ALM LANGUAGE TEXTBOOK

LEVEL I, Unit 2

**BASIC
DIALOGUE**

ON THE WAY TO THE LIBRARY

I

FITZWILLIAM: Hello, Janice, how are you?
JANICE: [Snubs him dead]

II

FITZWILLIAM: Say, Janice, are you on your way to the library?
JANICE: Look, can't you take a hint? Go bother somebody else. Please, just leave me alone.
FITZWILLIAM: I'm going there too. Shall we go together?
JANICE: Jesus!
FITZWILLIAM: Oh, look. There's a policeman. Let's ask directions of him.
JANICE: Will you just *go away*? Listen, my boyfriend is really going to—
FITZWILLIAM: Good morning, officer. I'd like you to meet Janice. She's been trying to sell me an ounce of cocaine.

III

FITZWILLIAM: I played a very practical joke on Janice this afternoon.
NED: Good. She's such a disagreeable youngster. Let's get down to the gritty-nitty. What hijinks did you play?
FITZWILLIAM: I spun a yarn that implied her guilt regarding contraband.
NED: Did you just blow that out your ass?
FITZWILLIAM: Even so. Now she'll dwell in the can for five to ten.
NED: Fine. Oh, look. It threatens to rain dogs and cats. Let's go inside and break your record player.

USEFUL PHRASES

In English, certain utterances occur with such great frequency that the student would be well advised simply to memorize them in their entirety. Each sentence should also be seen as a model representing the basic format of a whole class of similar utterances.

1. Yes-or-No questions: Do you think I like it when you wave your tits in his face?

2. Word questions: Why is Curt Gowdy famous?

3. exclamations: I can't believe how widespread oral sex is!

4. Hortatory exhortatives: And let's not bring up my little problem in front of the guests this time, okay?

5. Mendacious prevaricatives: But we can still be good friends, can't we?

6. Minatory relatives: I'll dance on your grave, Sis.

7. Vehicular guidance directives: Right. I mean "correct" — go left.

8. Cinemascopic preparatives: Why don't I let you get in line while I go park.

9. Paternal prophylactic Explanatives: They're balloons, but they're my balloons!

INTONATION DRILLS

In English the intonation of a sentence is often as important as the semantic content in expressing meaning. It would be a good idea to memorize the following sentences as models of the most basic intonation patterns of English assertions.

1. Simple declarative:

The lawn mower is in the shed.
2. Simple distress exclamation:
   The lawn mower is on my foot!
3. Complex distress exclamation:
   The lawn mower is in bed with my wife?

 # ITEM SUBSTITUTION DRILLS

Teacher	Student
1. Jack turns on the television.	Jack turns on the television.
(the sly)	Jack turns on the sly.
(a dime)	Jack turns on a dime.
(and on)	Jack turns on and on.
(red)	Jack turns on red.
(the authorities)	Jack turns on the authorities.
(to life)	Jack turns on to life.
(command)	Jack turns on command.
(Bridgit)	Jack turns on Bridgit.
2. Susan elapsed.	Susan elapsed.
(Jack)	Jack elapsed.
(liquidated all enemies foreign and domestic)	Jack liquidated all enemies foreign and domestic.
(liquidated all debts public and private)	Jack liquidated all debts public and private.
(liquidated all creatures great and small)	Jack liquidated all creatures great and small.
(caught rickettsia and grew reticent)	Jack caught rickettsia and grew reticent.

 # MISPRONUNCIATION DRILLS

In English, native speakers cultivate the following cute mispronunciations in their children, even though such errors will keep them out of the college of their choice.

athalete   coldslaw

chimbley
excape
liberry
mischievious
ellemenohpee

larynyx
menestration
nucular
Winsconsin
aksed

NOTE: The word "chimera" has no correct pronunciation in English.

 # COMPOUND PHRASES

In English, some phrases occur only as indivisible units, even though they appear to be constructed of discrete words. The following adjectives can only be used with the nouns paired with them. These phrases must be memorized. Do not attempt to make up your own phrases.

furtive glance
insurmountable odds
abject poverty
inexpressible grief
ineffable bliss
exorbitant prices
Joanne Woodward
senseless violence
luxuriant vegetation
gurgling stream
execrable taste

limpid pool
ebbing tide
charred body
venial sin
sordid affair
catlike quickness
lightning-quick reflexes
benign tumor
waning interest
pendulous breasts
grinding halt

DIALOGUE ADAPTATION

In the Pizza Parlor

CUSTOMER: Large pepperoni, please?

PIZZAIST: Yuh.
[ten-minute pause]

PIZZAIST: Large pepperoni.

CUSTOMER: Yuh.

parlor: chamber for reception of guests

large: gargantuan, Brobdingnagian

pizzaist: pizza operator

yuh: [here] I will make just that.

yuh: [here] I will claim that order, please.

Professor:—Henceforth, gentlemen, there will be 8000 pages of outside reading each week instead of 100.

There will also be frequent conferences for which I must require you to write a thesis on the syphonophor and its relation to the Morbid State of Rhode Island.

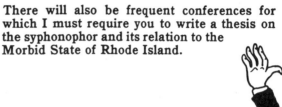

Furthermore, there will be tri-monthly visits to the Reformatory of Deer Isle for research purposes,

And I intend in the future to conduct this course in Lithuanian.

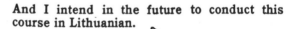

MUSIC
THE UNIVERSAL LANGUAGE

My last lecture pretty much covered art. Great art, I think we all agreed, is "anything we've all seen before." Now on to music.

I was originally going to lecture on "Opera — Overweight Lovers Starving in a Four-Story Garret," but that seems so unconscionably epigrammatic, and besides, so specific a topic lacks the listlessly broad scope required in a survey course like this one. So music at large it is. The whole aesthetic shebang.

Pencils poised?

Music is the universal language. Of course, you can't say anything really useful in it, like "apple pie and coffee," but it's as unparsable to a Finn as it is to a Chinaman, and that speaks for a brotherhood of sorts. Actually, and this will be on the examination, music *is* a language — insofar as its notes are actually seven letters of the known alphabet (to wit: A,B,C,D,E,F and, lastly, G).

"Now," you may well ask, "how does it help Mr. Talking Inclined-Man on the Street?" Mr. Willis, my teaching assistant, will demonstrate on these squeeze-bulb horns you see lined up here. Mr. Willis? To the horns, please.

So, it stands to reason that any words composed entirely of the letters A,B,C,D,E,F or G can be nonverbally expressed by emitting appropriate differently pitched honks. "CABBAGE" and "BAGGAGE" are two examples that spring to mind.

Handy for dining and traveling, those words.

So, virtually a third of the alphabetical canon can be alternately expressed by music.

Very good, Mr. Willis. That was "The C Major Scale," by Anonymous. No, Mr. Willis, I don't think we need to see the beach-ball balancing today.

But back to music as the universal language. The contrary listener will of course argue that to, say, a Spaniard — even a Spaniard keenly set to translate any musical notes he hears into words — these melodic meta-letters make no sense once collated. That is to say, "CABBAGE" holds no meaning for him. (Here I can't help remarking that, after all, the obstinate foreigner who has refused to learn English should shoulder a portion of the blame.) And for Japanese or Arabic *ecouteurs*, the coded letters themselves are alien.

As a means of communicating strictly in English, one must admit that speaking in music erases regional dialects altogether. No nasal Midwestern A sound will render the word bad, screechy or unpleasant, no matter how Ohioan the speaker, if he whistles the letter-note correspondents.

Does this limit our vocabulary? Perhaps. Research indicates that the pre-H words number about twenty-five. Among them: GAB, BED, FAD, DABBED, and BE.

While a twenty-five word selection seems serviceable to this observer, compared with the 170,000 words existing in English as it stands today, a sense of loss, however sentimental, is unavoidable. So, the switch to musical communication may not be in our lifetime, which scuttles my hopes for the system pretty roundly because I'm not going to have any children.

In my next lecture, "Underwater Immersion and the Creative Process," we will be examining the burst of artistic energy that often accompanies drowning, particularly energy directed toward the field of modern dance.

"I HAVE A TWENTY-PAGE PAPER DUE TOMORROW..."

"Complain, complain, that's all you ever do around here. C'mon, out with it. It's not really so bad, *n'est-ce pas? Quel* gives? Aaaaaaaah, let's see a little smile."

"Christ. Oh, Jesus Christ." *I just sit down to think in the privacy of my own brain for a few minutes when suddenly there you are, standing right in my own room bothering me with your stupid fat wet lips, you pig.*

"God, the attack of the *Cat People!* Well, *no offense!* Excuse me for breathing. God, just when somebody only wants to cheer somebody up, they turn into Little Miss Metaphysics her*self*. And it's my room too, don't forget. Or maybe you'd prefer for me to sleep out there in the trees? No, look. Y'okay? Want to talk about it? Go out for a beer or something? Whatever you want."

"I *have a twenty-page paper due tomorrow and I haven't done any of the reading for it plus I'm overdrawn thirty bucks. Now will you get out of here?*"

Thank you for getting out. Bang. Now you are dead. I shot you with my finger as you went out the door and I killed you. I have a single room now and I'll be able to get many hours of work done, even though it's 11:30 already. A closer examination of the clock, which has been placed very close to the typewriter so that I will worry more, reveals that in fact it is really 11:38, much too unprofessional a time for a serious student to begin work. It would probably be more useful to organize my thoughts until 12:00, and maybe to clean up my cluttered desk as well — can't work well in cluttered surroundings — and to water the plants. My desk is easily taken care of: a nest of unanswered letters, bills and crumbs is carefully shuffled and lined up neatly, exactly parallel to the desk's edge. (The secret to cleaning consists simply in placing everything at right angles and in straight lines. I am the only person who has thought of this.) Later the papers will be moved to the floor and lost. Then I find and eat a very old Lifesaver which was under some of the papers. Here is a fallen picture of my mother, wedged between the desk and the wall. Rereading some coffeed birthday cards —oh, yes, I did have a birthday once, when people loved me, before they left me working all alone in the night — and looking for tape for the picture take up three minutes, by which time one of the plants has dripped dirty water onto my typing paper and some overdue reference books, and now it is 12:05. Time to make a few phone calls and to play one side of a good, peppy album that'll really get me in the mood to work. And then I accidentally fall asleep on the sofa until 3:30.

Several things disquiet me when I wake up. Not the least of these is the fact that I now have only seven hours to work, but the smear of caked drool from the corner of my mouth down to my chin also does its share. I can see a small pool of same on the sofa where my mouth was, and the phrase "pool of drool, pool of drool" will keep me company for the rest of the night, certainly. What an interesting person I am! In addition, one of my legs is fatally twisted from having been slept on wrong, and one of my eyes is sealed shut. And now the birds are waking up outside! Maybe one will fly in here and I can tame it.

A pallid dawn leaks through the curtains once "work" is finally in process. By now, of course, the notion that reference books, notes or syntax are important has melted away, and I am writing in medieval French. This is not so surprising: archaic languages evolved in direct proportion to their ease in being typed, and many vowel combinations which we now consider obsolete make sense, when you think about them, for they enable us to type much faster and so increase production output. The fact that I stop work after thirteen pages rather than the assigned twenty to twenty-five also speeds up the process considerably. "Pith over pages" might be my motto here, and I decide to add a note of wry humor to the paper by typing the slogan at its last sentence (the section man is nice and will like the joke lots, if I'm not mistaken).

Someone, probably my roommate, has stolen the stapler from its hiding place under the refrigerator, and I am forced to bind the finished work with three bobby pins. That done, I have no alternative but to begin proofreading the first page of my junior thesis. There is very little hope of my going dyslexic now.

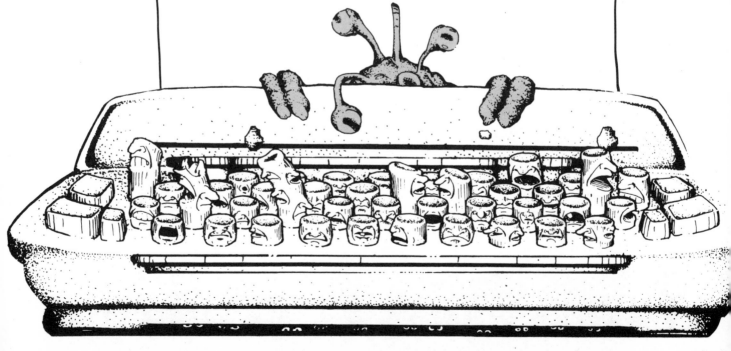

Located in the Andres are the ruins of ann
Injan civilization fames for it's brick-engraved
poettery. Upon examination, this potery at firs,
hoever, seemed difficult to study, for one examining
it, we find that the sharks of potttery don't hole
up wall when being exposed. to bright sunfight.

REVIEW SESSION

Once in the late 1960s a senior at U. Cal. Berkeley named George J. Sanders and a junior named Jennifer A. Walker studied together for a progressive course entitled Images of Protest and made more academic progress than they could have achieved independently over the same stretch of time. It is the only recorded instance of academic success having accrued from such a collaboration. The other seven and a half billion attempts went more like this:

GIRL: I'm so worried about this test — I feel like I'm in junior high.

BOY: I know.

GIRL: And I really know the material. I mean I know the material but I just can't answer any questions about it, you know?

BOY: Yeah, I know. I think a graded test in sociology is a contradiction in terms anyway. I mean, A's and B's are just labels society arbitrarily fastens to papers with correct answers on them.

GIRL: I really don't care anymore. How can you keep this stuff straight? Alcoholism *is* a disease, homosexuality isn't — I just don't know anymore. Oh, and what are the three goals of life? I keep forgetting.

BOY: Oh, it's self-actualization, self-preservation . . . and . . . jeez . . .

GIRL: Compassion?

BOY: No . . . that was last semester, I'll have to look that up.

GIRL: Oh well. Then could you explain what that thing was about the development of modernity? I missed that lecture.

BOY: Well, I think the whole development of modernity can be traced in skeletal form in Louis Malle's latest film. It's about a roller coaster ride through war-torn France — it's called *Ouiiiii*. Did you see it? I really think it's his best. He has such a sense of the movie as cinema. Perhaps I just found it personally very easy to identify with the hero — especially the part when he has his first affair. I remember back to my first . . . "experience" — way back — ah, how we loved one another. We loved each other on so many different levels.

GIRL: Did you have a bunk bed?

BOY: Have you ever . . . I don't want to say "gone steady" with someone — I mean, this is the seventies after all — but did you ever, like, go with a guy . . . steadily?

GIRL: Well, I was married once.

BOY: Because I think it's an experience essential to the maturation process that you can't substitute anything else for. When I think of the evenings we spent together, driving around discussing our futures, choosing our favorite houses, trying to get the stains off the glove compartment . . . she was a rare one. But you don't want to hear about her.

GIRL: No. . . no, I don't. But it's a very moving story. What ever happened to her?

BOY: I went over there one evening and we had this political discussion. Ah, she

was a Trotskyite and I was Socialist Labor; it was silly to have ever dreamt it could have worked.

GIRL: Maybe a drink would cheer you up.

BOY: Sure . . . shall I flip a little something on the rotogravure?

GIRL: Sure. [He sits down closer to her.] I like your Liberate Angola button.

BOY: Thanks. Would you like a granola bar? It's a nutritious snack.

GIRL: Oh, thank you. Mmmm, they're like candy bars . . . without the taste.

BOY: [After a pause] Maybe you'd like some downers? I've got some quaaludes.

GIRL: No, thanks — I get low on life .

BOY: You're beautiful when you're neoconservative.

GIRL: [Embarrassed at the compliment] Oh, thank you . . . but it's just that I'm a little cautious about certain things.

BOY: A little cautious? You want to marry a banker, you want a house in the suburbs, you don't like Volvos, John Coltrane, or yogurt.

GIRL: Well, I admit I'm not a flaming radical. I worry about the future. I mean, when I'm forty I want to be able to live comfortably. I don't want to have to live hand to mouth, wondering where my next down vest is coming from. What are you going to do with yourself after graduation?

BOY: Oh, I don't know . . . travel a little . . . maybe write a little . . . *live* a little, you know? Like a guy I knew who died recently — an itinerant artist of sorts — his whole life was his work of art. He was improverished, a hobo, an addict.

GIRL: How did he die?

BOY: It was tragic. He hang-glided into some power lines. What a statement.

GIRL: But he's dead.

BOY: Yeah. . . I think I see your problem. You're having trouble reconciling the concepts of living fully and being dead.

GIRL: Yes, I think that's it.

BOY: I think maybe you're just more function oriented than I am. You judge people by how they fulfill a function in society, and you can't understand the value of someone who doesn't even fulfill his vital functions. I, on the other hand, feel that a man is most fully human when he's not functioning at all.

GIRL: Well, there doubtless is a functional component of my mind, but there's also a large completely nonfunctional part.

BOY: Well, I wish that were so, but I can't really —

GIRL: Oh, I see. [Angry pause.]

BOY: [Conciliatory] But that can be good too. There are some good functions that ought to be fulfilled. [Silence] Copulation! [**GIRL** is startled; **BOY** hastily explains] That was the third goal of life — self-actualization, self-preservation and copulation.

GIRL: Oh, of course. That's all three all right. Well, I guess I'm ready then . . . for the test . . . [Rising to go] tomorrow.

BOY: Good, good. [Both are reluctant, but neither is courageous enough to stop the other.]

GIRL: Well, take care.

BOY: Sweet dreams.

December, 1978   **Final Examination**   Professor Wilhelm

English A

Literature From The Beginning To The Present

I.(60 Minutes.) Match each of the quotations below with the
correct author from the list at the end of the section.   Then
discuss why you think each of your choices is correct, and
finally analyze the complete work from which the quotation is
excerpted.

1. Arma virumque Cano, Troiae qui primus ab oris...

2. Whan that Aprille with his shoures soote
   The droght of March hath perced to the roote...

3. To be or not to be: that is the question.

4. St. Agnes' Eve--Ah, bitter cold it was!
   The owl, for all his feathers, was a-cold...

5. The teargas drifted up to the Vice
           President naked in the bathroom
   --naked on the toilet taking a shit weeping?
   Who wants to be President of the
           Garden of Eden?

A. Chaucer, The Canterbury Tales. B. Shakespeare, Hamlet.
C. Keats, "St. Agnes' Eve." D. Ginsberg, The Fall of America.
E. Vergil, The Aeneid.

II. (60 Minutes.) It has been suggested by literary critics and
other smart thinkers that many of the great writers have dealt
with identical themes. Agree or disagree, using at least FOUR
of the themes listed below and ELEVEN of the following writers:
Seneca, Rabelais, Wyatt, Spenser, Herrick, Swift, Feydeux,
Austen, Goethe, Joyce, Malraux, Nin and Doctorow.

THEMES: Death, Knowledge, Life, Love, Religion, Society.

III. (60 Minutes; 10 Minutes per question recommended.)

1. Discuss imagery in Elizabethan and Renaissance literature,
   with at least some reference to Paradise Lost, Paradise
   Regained, Donne, Herbert, Marvell, Vaughan and Jacobean drama.

2. Briefly compare 19th Century to 20th Century literature.

3. What do you think drives people to create works of great
   literary achievement? Discuss, also giving examples from
   the worlds of painting, music and science.

4. Detail some of the differences between prose and poetry
   and decide which is a better form. Be sure to discuss the novel.

5. Trace the development of drama from Aristophanes to LeRoi Jones.

6. Briefly compare French to English Literature, with some
   reference to other literatures(German, Italian, Greek, African,
   American) as well.

December, 1978   Final Examination   Professor Condor

Intellectual History 1350a

Read over the entire examination before starting to answer questions.
This test is designed to last two hours and 50 minutes. This will allow
you 3 minutes to wonder whether or not the proctor said you could begin
yet, 2 minutes to decide whether or not you should actually read over
the entire test before starting, and five minutes to get a head start on
those who decide to read it over.

1. (60 minutes) Wrench twelve of the writers we have studied from context
   and cram their divergent theses into the Procrustean bed of a single
   coherent theme. Abandon any vestigial intellectual integrity or
   lingering sense of self in an attempt to bow to your grader's every
   whim. Conclude with a frenetic attempt to use more space while intro-
   ducing nothing new, preferably a paraphrasis of your topic sentence.
   Do not forget to scrawl "Time" at the bottom of your last page.

2. (30 minutes) Agree with the following proposition from my upcoming book:

      "Intellectual history can scarcely be regarded as a be-all;
      rather, we must view it as an end-all."

3. (50 minutes) Write on ONE of the following two topics:

   A. Trace the development of one fatuous concept through three thinkers
      until a fourth expresses the culmination of that concept and yet,
      in a way, simultaneously sounds its death knell. Incorporate at
      least two specious parallels between these thinkers' worldviews,
      one of which should be based on your cursory glance at the exam
      period assignment.

   B. (Students in the Applied Intellectualism Section MUST answer B.)
      Suppose you are at a party and some vapid asshole begins sidling
      in on your date with a coherent theory of why contemporary French
      fiction has been staging a comeback since the early 1960's.
      Counter with a spurious argument constructed from a misreading of
      the major texts we have explored this semester; you should make
      a tenuous analogy to contemporary film, employ the terms mise-en-
      scene and "social milieu," and close by having no choice but to
      summarily dismiss his views, while conceding that your own
      interpretation must seem somewhat heretical to someone of his
      traditional mindset.

4. (30 minutes) Ramble for several bluebooks about the headlong strides
   being scored every day in quelling one of the social injustices which
   have been spreading like a cancerous growth on the ship of our state.
   While bird-dogging this issue from both the research data/input angle
   and the multiple output/result characteristics angle, be sure and
   include several pages on process methodology technique. In the late
   innings, see if you can't get a bead on using "target" and "impact"
   as transitive verbs and "turn around" as a noun, while occasionally
   touching base with homey metaphors drawn from the world of sport;
   be sure and include at least two pleonastic gaffs to solely annoy
   Edwin Newman and his switch-hitting teammates. If you want to beef up
   your conclusion as you reach the finish line, set your sights on
   the paper of the troubleshooter sitting beside you and let him do a
   little unwitting pinch-hitting.

Section

4

Enter
The
Serpent:
Activities
And
Social
Life

VANITAS

College? Sure, I been to college. It's just like high school, only more dames wear glasses and fewer shave their legs. The books I could live without. It's the social environment — you know, the boy meets girl, boy makes girl think he's Einstein, boy gets girl part — that's really my concern. And that's what I want to talk to you about.

Now a lot of you little weenies out there probably figure the scene at college is just like those brochure things make it out to be — nude Frisbee contests, topless study sessions and free petting during lectures. Well, hold on, buckaroo, because to begin with 80 percent of college women are lesbos, and the other 20 percent spend all their time reading foreign editions of books written in English. If you want the straight dope, just listen up and stop playing with your slide rules or you'll wind up dating a line of Texas Instruments calculators.

I should warn you of something first. I happen to be an incredible stud. Perhaps "make-out artist" is a better term. I've been chewing face ever since I can remember — in drive-ins, bowling alley and restaurant booths, over a few frosties, some burgers or maybe a Clark bar or two. I've used props every now and then, sure: wax lips, tongue depressors, plastic vampire teeth, the usual. As far as I'm concerned, once you've gotten to first base there's nowhere left to go.

Yeah, I know a lot of you guys were figuring once you got to *college* you'd go for the "big time": goosing, copping feels, nipple gnawing, dry humping, and having your inseam measured by some Candice Bergen type. To me, a healthy exchange of mucus through oral contact is unbeatable. I tried a lot of heavy stuff before settling down to necking as my life's ambition. I sprayed Water Pics into ears, wore wet suits in bed, the whole deal, but it all seemed so artificial, so trite. There's no future in polymorphous perversity. (As you can see, I've done some research into the matter.) I've said it before, so I'll tell you geeks one more time before you start hugging a card catalog: making out is the purest form of pleasure permissible in Western civilization.

And they love it. I don't care how smart they are or how many times they've done obscure Scandinavian Double-Crostics. I haven't met a chick yet who could resist getting some tongue. As soon as you get near them, they're shutting their blinkers and shooting open their yappers as if they're waiting for the *Queen Mary* to sail in. If you just watch them eating or talking sometime, you can tell that what they really want is a juicy, sloppy hot soul kiss. Why do you think they're always gabbing away so much? Because they have anything to say? Christ, no; it's advertising. Maybe these crazy broads go for spit transfusions or something, but they're just tongue-tanks as far as I can see.

Well, anyway, to get back to this so-called social life you get at these colleges, let me tell you this unbelievable story about this date I once had at school. I used to cruise the nursing school a lot, because that's where the real Grade A, USDA-inspected meat used to hang out and probably still does, while the by-products all major in Flemish linguistics or something. The only ones easier to score with than nurses are your roommates' girlfriends, but they're usually busy telling your roommates how sorry they are and how they'll never do it again.

So there was this nursing student I had the hot huey for — you know, the real wild wadango and all — so I finally asked her out one night. I took her on the usual tantalizing tour of the off-campus love stations: some miniature golf, a few frames of pins, a short stop at the driving range and then some pizza. Everything was going great, and I could tell by the way she kept wiping off her mouth with her elbow that she was just begging for a little lip limbering. The only problem was that I had this enormous cold sore which I had been picking at all night so it was oozing pus and everything all down my chin. It must have been really gross.

So I take her back to her room, and I'm waiting to hear her tell me to take a powder or wipe the drool off my cheeks or whatever, but instead she invites me inside. By this time I was dribbling like mad, and my sore was excreting all over my shirt, and I was nearly losing my cool, when she puts on some Led Zep record and starts running her hands over my body. I couldn't figure her out for the life of me. I chalked her up as a whacko and decided I might as well give her what she wanted while I was at it. I gave my face one last cleansing with my sleeve and started sliding into the paydirt.

After about an hour or so of heavy slurping on the saliva surf, I told her I had to go to my room and repaint the fire door. She wanted more, but I knew what was on her mind, so I bagged her. It just goes to show — when you get right down to it they don't care if you look like Cary Grant or Lon Chaney. It's a dirty business, and it doesn't matter if you're covered with mud. So what I'm telling you gobblers who're already wasting your time putting reinforcements on the pages in your notebooks is that if you just don't get carried away, you can have as good a time at college as you did in high school. Only remember: Watch out for this "mature relationship" garbage or you'll be reading *Ms.* magazine while washing your girlfriend's black lace support hose. And stay away from the ones who haven't been outside since somebody pulled the fire alarm at the main library. Think tongue and you'll go a long way.

RESSIONISTIC Byron Hero

OST New Criticism HARLEM

ODERN NEGATIVE RENAISSA

etic ISM CAPABILITY LITERARY
DECADENCE

TONE CONTEXTUALISM pre·raphaelite

POEM TRAGÉDIE Mock·Heroic
CLASSIQUE Intentional Falla

OBJECTIVE CORRELATIVE

YELLOW NOVEL

Synesthesia

FAKING IT

Okay, so maybe you've blown dope with Bowie, been a three-time All-American, invented a new death bomb or bought every Coltrane disc ever pressed. But face it, Jack, when the talk turns to the Big Books, you're up dumbo creek. You skip the hippest *haute kultur* happenings on campus, avoid those beautiful brainy babes and probably spend most of Saturdays saying to yourself, "Damn, if only I knew what 'objective correlative' meant and how it relates to Wordsworth's 'dark poems,' I could *really* be having some fun!"

Well, now you can, and you won't even have to sit in the library like a big wiener all day. By following the advice you are about to read, you"ll be cutting the literary mustard with the best of them and bedding down the buxom Comp. Lit. majors before you can say "anapestic hexameter."

I. SOME GENERAL RULES

Always assume that everyone else is faking it to some extent. Even your basic professor types have read maybe 30 percent of what they pretend to. Which brings us to the second cardinal rule:

Never talk about well-known books. Most of these English major sorts have actually had to read the really famous books at some point. Talk instead about the "neglected minor masterpieces." If the author in question is a poet, talk about his unpublished prose, and vice versa. Also feel free to invent material which you "found in his notebooks in a deserted part of the rare books library."

Never say that you recently "read" a book. This is very, very important. Literary heavyweights never read books. They *re*read them.

We're now ready to move on to the specific pointers that will speed you on your way to bookish prowess.

II. GLOSSARY

Hesse, Brautigan, Vonnegut: Writers you read when you were in high school, before you outgrew them. Verbally destroy anyone over the age of eighteen who mentions them. Example: "Do you believe it? The man's twenty-two years old and still thinks *Steppenwolf* is a masterpiece!"

Beowulf: The only thing you need to know is that despite the title, there is no wolf in the story. You can also say that the translations are universally abysmal, and you are considering one of your own.

Shakespeare: The biggie. Everybody knows something about Shakespeare; the trick is knowing what to mention and what to ignore. Never, never under any circumstances discuss *Julius Ceasar, Macbeth* or *Othello,* which are only read and studied in high school. Only speak of *Hamlet* in terms of "the paradox of Hamlet" (a neat phrase meaning any type of existential confusion) or when comparing your roommate's bad acid trip with Orphelia's mad scene.

Always use the definitive article when referring to the types of plays: *the* Histories, *the* Tragedies, etc. Also use contradictory adjectives to describe them, as in "the dark Comedies," "the happy Tragedies," "the cynical Romances" and "the inaccurate Histories." Be aware of the fact that there are at least three plays which nobody has ever read: *Titus Andronicus, King John* and *The Winter's Tale.* Feel free to attribute random lines or sayings to these plays. In the same vein, even world-famous Shakespeare scholars cannot keep the names of all those kings and queens straight so you can talk confidently about such nonexistent plays as *Thomas II, Edward III* or *James IV.* Be careful, though: a reference to the production you just saw of *Donald the Twelfth* may draw some disbelieving stares. Should anyone question you, swiftly reply, "Oh excuse me, that was his working title for the third draft of *The Merry Wives of Windsor.*"

Politics: Boring with a capital B. Some good responses when the topic is introduced: "Politics is the poetry of the spiritually and aesthetically impoverished" or "There are no political solutions, only artistic dilemnas." If you must register some ideological affiliation, say that you were a Trotskyite until you reread some mistranslated passages from his unpublished notebooks.

Magazines: Outhip the hipsters by saying that you do not bother to read such voguish publications as *The New Yorker, The Atlantic* and *The New York Review of Books.* Accuse each one of having "succumbed to the Me generation/*People* magazine phenomenon." If pressed about any other periodical, say that you canceled your subscription when it changed graphic designers.

French Names: Don't try pronouncing any that you aren't sure of, feel free to make some up. Talk about Moineau's latest novel, Belfleur's theory of aesthetics or Detrop's article that you didn't bother to read in *The Paris Review.* Try it: Flanpeur. Drachmont. Presquetourne. See how easy it is?

Other foreign words and phrases: Pick up any dictionary and memorize the list of foreign expressions listed at the back, paying special attention to the ones for which there are perfectly good English idioms already. Why use the vulgar "When the cat's away, the mice will play!" when you can casually drop identical "Via il gatto ballano I sorci!" Reply to knotty questions with irrelevant foreign quips. If you are asked about Cowper's use of the semicolon, slyly point out that "a chi has testa, non manca capello" (a man with a head will not be without a hat). When questioned about the finer points of Paul Tillich's doctrines, smile knowingly and mutter, "Gutta cavat lapidem; consumitur annulus usu" (dripping water hollows the rock; the ring is worn away by use).

Pets peeves: Arbitrarily pick one well-respected poet (a list of these can be found in many reference books) and wage a personal vendetta against him. Whenever his work is mentioned, hurl your drink against the wall and scream, "The man's a fraud! A complete fake!"

Should anyone have the temerity to challenge your opinion, smile condescendingly and say, "Oh, come on now. You just go back and reread one of his so-called poems. It's obvious!" You can establish a reputation and a cachet in this way. It is better to be known on the cocktail circuit as "the one who loathes Dryden" than as "the one who drinks too much."

III. SOME SAMPLE USES

Before we get carried away with ourselves, let's remember what it is that you're after. You're learning to talk like some pansy Einstein because you're looking for a warm place to nest your love leaflet, and we're not talking about some cozy corner of the library. The sole object of faking it is to impress the hell out of women who will then follow you home before you can say "negative capability."

Let's assume you're at some typical literary-type cocktail party and you espy a comely lass (pick out a looker) across the room. Here are some ways you can break the ice with your newfound skills:

YOU: Did you hear what the so-called professor was saying about Freud's influence on Keats? Any child knows that the Continental translations betrayed a *jus sufragii!*
SHE: How true!
YOU: Charltans like that probably still believe that intercourse is the way to please a woman! Say, I have some monographs back in my room...
YOU: Have you read Eaudechien's commentaries on *Richard V* lately?
SHE: Er...ah, yes, yes I have.
YOU: Laden with *sturm und drang,* wouldn't you say?
SHE: You're very smart. Let's have sexual relations.

IV. CONCLUSION

With your new mastery of intellectual discourse, you should have no problems whatsoever re-creating scenes such as the ones described above.

There are a couple of final pointers you fellows should keep in mind. There are two special circumstances which may throw you for a loop. You may, once in your lifetime, actually meet someone who really *is* as smart as you are only pretending to be.[1] He has read everything ever written and often speaks knowledgeably and eloquently. Do not try to fake it with such a person. Instead, engage him in conversation about baseball, construction work, the quality of cheap brands of bourbon or the size of women's breasts. For some reason, intellectuals think it fashionable to discuss such things with one another.

You may also run into someone who is up to exactly the same thing you are. Don't panic: this is a stroke of the highest fortune. Engage in screaming arguments with him over specious points in full view of everyone else, and arrange together that you will always say that the other has the finest mind you have ever run across. With any luck, you should both be full professors by the time you're thirty.

[1]Besides me, there are six such people in the United States and none in Central or South America.

THE AMOROUS CURRICULUM

With the unhurried ease of a vagrant false eyelash floating serenely toward the frothy top of a prom queen's second brandy Alexander, spring has come to the university. Fitting, isn't it, that spring should be the season for the release of the long-awaited "Report to the President on the Amorous Curriculum?" The committee's 600-plus-page report was delivered last week and selected portions are reprinted below.

FROM THE INTRODUCTION

"We find it appalling that romance and sexual love, highly important facets of undergraduate life, have in the past been handled so haphazardly by the college. We have devised a varied and highly challenging system of options for study in the romantic discipline. We are confident that the achievement-oriented student will respond well to the competitive character of the program."

OPTION NUMBER ONE: "The Hapless, Callow Youth"

Only a basic program is available under this option. After the first three weeks of each term, students who elect this option are required to submit a list of no fewer than three but no more than five names of members of the college whom they will desire passionately, but never speak to for the rest of the year. The student concentrating in amorous Option Number One must demonstrate an appropriately torturous frequency of exposure to each loved one on his or her list (in dining halls, classes, libraries, etc.) before that list may be approved. A short (3 to 5 page) paper is required of all students in this option. In the paper, the student is expected to present and embellish a fantasy involving one of his loved ones.

> **SAMPLE:** "When I caught up with her, Marcia was in repose against the rail of a rustic bridge. She laughed as a stray, warm breeze billowed the hem of her sleeveless summer dress. Her dark brown eyes telegraphed the signal that bosky frolic was about to commence. She beckoned me to move closer with a sumptuously tanned arm," etc.

Obviously, sex is never to rear its ugly little head in concentration number one. When it does, the involved student will be asked to transfer out of the program's jurisdiction.

OPTION NUMBER TWO: "The Pre-Professional Tryst"

This is an honors-only option open only to students intent on admission to highly competitive graduate schools. The program's administration office will help match and mate students preferably, but not necessarily, sharing the same all-consuming pre-professional interest. The couple must take at least two classes per term together, and must take MCAT's and LSAT's while seated at adjacent desks. The program office will also offer guidance to couples on the planning of recreation and wholesome nightlife. An engagement party is expected of all Option Two students in the spring of their senior year.

OPTION NUMBER THREE: "Everyone Else Sucks"

A non-honors program with strong ties to Option Two. Students who elect this option are required to eat every meal together, spend every weekend together, elect the same field of academic concentration, take at least three courses per semester together and sleep together every night in a cruelly undersized bed of college issue. Option Three students are also expected to loathe each other by the spring term of their senior year.

OPTION NUMBER FOUR: "Let's Stay Friends"

Open to mature sophomores and juniors who have forged deeply meaningful "friendships" with members of the opposite sex which would only be spoiled and complicated by the emotional mess that always accompanies sex. Recommended for the masochistic faction of the student body. Highest distinction is won by a gallant attempt at pushing Platonism to its outer limits. For instance, departmental citations are awarded to members of an Option Four couple who pass four or more chaste nights per term lying naked beside each other on one of those cruelly undersized college beds.

OPTION NUMBER FIVE: "The Grownup Affair"

Open to honors seniors and juniors concentrating in the humanities. The program office will pair male students who don't speak to anyone in the dining rooms and who carry around French paperbacks with a member of a small group of semibeautiful, thirtyish, divorced women living on modest trust funds in one-room walkups. These women must be currently engaged in the composition of their first sonnet sequences or confessional novels. They promise to view their younger partners as exquisite embodiments of innocent vitality. They are prone, in the midst of sexual congress, to shout out things like "Onward, ever onward, my lusty young Ganymede." It is strongly recommended that students in the English Department's writing option complete two of these liaisons before the submission of the senior thesis.

Females who elect this option are referred to the secretaries of the various academic departments, who keep lists of faculty members willing to participate in the program.

UNDER NO CIRCUMSTANCES WILL CREDIT BE GRANTED FOR WORK DONE IN THIS FIELD AT OTHER INSTITUTIONS.

FROM THE PAGES OF READER'S DIGEST

Campus Comedy

MY SON HAD BEEN SEEING the campus psychiatrist because of a mental illness. The sessions were expensive, though, so Jim decided to find part-time employment. Entering the company's office, he was astounded to find several dozen young men who apparently wanted the same job. Hours later, Jim was finally ushered in to meet the interviewer, a gruff-looking man in a conservative gray suit. Fixing a steely gaze on my son, the prospective employer sternly demanded: "Why should I hire you?"

Jim thought for a moment, then calmly answered, "Because I'm crazy, and if you don't I'll rip out your spinal cord and strangle you with it."

He got the job.

—MRS. H. PENNY (*Pleasantville, W. Va.*)

MY SON, THE POPULAR MUSIC NUT, was home from college when some workmen came to fix the family furnace. Soon the clanging of sledgehammers and the screeching of electric drills reverberated through the house. Unaware of the source of the noisy din, Mark turned to his friend and yelled, "Wow, what a far-out new rock combo!" He thought the noise was music from a "groovy" new rock group.

—MAGGIE ZEAN (*Happyton, Neb.*)

MY ROOMMATE, a perennial weight-watching husband-hunter who also likes to knit potholders, came up with a nifty reminder not to eat so darn much. She posted the following wry notice on the refrigerator; "Big and chubby means no get hubby." It was written on a potholder.

—PATTY MELT (*Smilesburg, Pa.*)

MY DAUGHTER FANCIES HERSELF something of a "child prodigy" on the violin. One day she and her roommate at college were doggedly practicing a concerto when who should walk in but Leonard Bernstein, the famous conductor! Seeing their good fortune, the two plucky young coeds improvised a beautiful rendition of Toscanini's "Il Duce Mio" just to impress the Hebrew band leader. When they were through with the piece, they looked to Mr. Bernstein with great expectation in their eyes. But he had already left. He's very busy.

—MRS. BUNNY PUPPY (*Chuckleville, Ind.*)

AS A PROFESSOR I generally don't approve of sex on the campus, but when two sparrows decided to "set up housekeeping" on our doorstep one fine spring morning, we just couldn't say no. Soon the birds became famous, and people came from almost a mile around just to ogle at the "love birds," as they were called. And when Mrs. Bird gave birth to six shiny new eggs, we were as happy as could be.

Unfortunately, we forgot to tell our little daughter, Peggy, and one morning she woke up early and decided to fix us breakfast. Stepping out to the front door for the eggs and dairy products the milkman had left for us, she unwittingly took the six sparrow eggs as well. We ate the eggs, and then went out to check on our feathered friends. Mr. and Mrs. Bird had fled—but not before scrawling this bill in the dirt: "Half a Dozen Eggs—50¢ please."

It just goes to show you: even the birds are suffering from inflation.

—PROFESSOR JENSEN *(Birdyton, Colo.)*

JUST BEFORE ELECTION DAY our local college sponsored a debate between the incumbent governor and a socialist who was popular with the disruptive element. My son, the budding campus radical, decided to hurl an egg at the governor as he delivered his speech. Imagine his chagrin when the eggy missile completely missed the governor and splattered directly in his favorite candidate's face!

—TINY BULL *(Lawnmow, Mich.)*

OUR FOOTBALL TEAM was undefeated going into its final game with the Jinxton Jumbos. Just before the kickoff, our archrivals uncaged their mascot, a pudgy baby elephant, and led him to the sidelines. Early in the first quarter, it became clear that "Jumbie" was no disinterested bystander. During our key plays, he would trumpet lustily, ruining our team's concentration. At halftime, trailing 14-0, things looked grim.

Finally, some of us hit on a novel way to silence the partisan pachyderm. While our rivals were still in the locker-room, my teammates and I forced several dozen footballs down Jumbie's throat with a down marker. The trick worked. He obviously wasn't happy, but the little elephant didn't make a peep for the remainder of the game. Shortly after we won, the feisty mascot suffocated, and excited fans tore his skin off. Then there was a big fight.

—MIKE MARK *(Caring, Minn.)*

DURING MY LAST YEAR at State my theology professor gave us a somewhat unorthodox final exam. He asked us to answer just one question: "How do you know that God exists?"

Amid furrowed brows and scribbling pens, I launched into a lengthy, detailed essay citing numerous renowned theologians. Glancing at the clock, I noticed a member of the football squad who appeared to be stumped. Throughout most of the hour, he frowned over his paper, unable to formulate an answer. Then, suddenly brightening, he scrawled something and handed in his exam in the nick of time.

My curiosity got the better of me, and I took a peek at what he had written. It consisted of just two words: "Niagara Falls."

He failed the course.

—COLE BEER *(Party Beach, Calif.)*

THE BIG GAME

It was 1956. Ike had just been re-elected. It was third down and twenty to go on our own twenty in the last game of the season, the game for the championship, The Big Game against Great State. Little Davey Baker, the third-string halfback, warmed the bench while his father warmed the bleachers. Charles Baker had never seen Davey play; he was blind. The old codger had come out to every game nonetheless, but his maladroit offspring had never seen action. He kept hoping that Coach Hass might let his Davey play, just for a minute, and that today might be that day.

Suddenly and without warning, a lone woman began shrieking hysterically from the stands. Davey and his gridiron buddies wheeled about and saw the elder Baker lying slumped against a fatty fan to his left. While a concerned crowd gathered, Davey sprang into action on the field, grabbing the ball and speeding eighty yards for a touchdown. The swift youngster crossed the goal-line just as the final gun fired and The Big Game ended at the same moment as Charles Baker's life.

Amid the roaring crowd, Davey trotted back to Coach Hass. "Is my Pop alright? asked the littlest halfback. "I'm sorry," said Coach Hass, "but your father is dead. "That's okay," the peewee replied goodnaturedly, "I know that he saw me from the great bleacher in the sky."

Sound familiar? Of course not. Football usually isn't like that and I ought to know. I'm Coach Hass. But stranger things have happened. Take our last Big Game just this past season. Sit down, 'cause you're not going to believe this.

Used to be, all my boys were smart, wore low-heeled shoes and drove compact cars, but what with the colored and everything that's happened in the last twenty years all I get now is a rainbow of trouble. The professor types try to make it easy for them, but you can only do so much. The week before this year's Big Game, Professor Burnburg was examining my star quarterback, who needed a passing grade to play in the championship contest.

"Name a zoo," the inquisitive Zoologist queried. The all-conference player looked hopefully to the ceiling for inspiration, then ventured after a pause, "Children's Zoo." The kindly but now red-faced pedagogue shook his head and tried anew.

"Perhaps you could name an animal," implored the well-read geriatric. For a silent half-minute the sports prodigy proved he could not. "Baa-baa," hinted the professor sheepishly. "Moo-moo," he offered helpfully. Still silence filled the room.

"Milkshake?" suggested the burly footballer.

To make a long story short, I had to start my second-string quarterback in the Big Game. As if that wasn't enough, the fatboys up in the Dean's office have been riding gunshot on my butt all season about letting women use the field. Two days before the Big Game, Dean "Ms." Smythe kicked us off the turf so that some split-bellies could practice their lesbian cosmetic training.

Somehow I got my crew of cripples and idiots suited up for the Big Game and it seemed for a while that luck had strapped on a helmet with them. It was like a crazy dream until the fourth quarter, when we fell apart and let in four touchdowns to fall two points behind. With the ball in our own territory in the final minute, we ran an off-tackle out of the wishbone and got pegged for a big loss, leaving us close to our own goal-line and our second-string QB with a broken collarbone. I called time-out to speak with the dazed youth. "We'd be okay," he said, shaking with each word, "if only we could disintegrate that space being. It's not fair..."

"Snap out of it!" I demanded, brutally slapping the injured youngster back into semi-consciousness. With precious seconds left in the time-out I made a last-ditch attempt to win, but before I could force the needle into his brain a loud uproar resounded through the stands. As the security police bludgeoned a path through the crowd, the body of a supine spectator became visible. It was Davey Baker, the star of the Big Game twenty-two years earlier.

Davey was croaking in the bleachers just as his old man had done. Suddenly little Mickey Baker, Davey's son, ran up to me and stammered, "C-C-Coach, you wanna get lucky?" It was history repeating itself. The cards were in my favor. Little Mickey was going to do it for his old man. We were going to win the Big Game.

A hush fell over the crowd as the ball was snapped. Then, bodies clashed, bones crashed, a lone dog howled, women fainted, and people screamed. When the dust had cleared, the only one left standing was little Mickey. He hurtled over a pile of human debris and sprinted to glory. I was already deciding what to wear to the victory banquet when Mickey tripped four yards short of the goal-line, sending the ball flying yards behind him. Players from both teams smothered the pigskin as the gun fired ending the game. We had lost.

Mickey trotted sadly back to the bench. With tears in his eyes, he asked, "Coach, how's my Pop?" I placed a finger under his chin, lifted his head, looked into his eyes and smiled. "He's dead—loser."

Do You Want to Be MORE POPULAR?

She's smart, she's confident, she radiates energy and cheer. She's turned on by exciting people, places and ideas — the kind only a top-notch school can provide. Most of all, she has something to say — and when she says it, people listen.

How does Kristi do it? Ask friends who surround her, if you can pull them away! They'll tell you that she does drugs. Hard drugs. The rugged, durable, we-mean-business drugs that only the folks at Benzene Labs can give you. Because we care.

You see, we're the only people who deal strictly to students. That means if you want "red devils," "blue demons," "yellow sunshine" or any other showy pill — head straight to our competitors. They're good people too. But if you're looking for honest amphetamines at a modest cost — from crosses to crystal — then come to us. That's why we're here.

BENZINE LABORATORIES
SINCE 1927

SEX ON CAMPUS

INTRODUCTION

Due to the increasing availability and use of sex on college campuses, accompanied by recent federal legislation reducing the penalties for possession of sexual objects (note: penalties for engaging in the profitable exchange and/or manufacture of said objects remain quite stringent), University Health Services feels that it is in the best interests of all involved to offer pertinent information on the all too frequently misunderstood topic of sex use and abuse. Overindulgence in sexual activities has left society to care for a growing population of "sex addicts" — persons requiring a daily "fix" of sex. Then there is the danger of "overdosing," or death caused by the consumption of an inordinate amount of consummation. It is our opinion that the more facts of sex use that are brought to light, the more easily these hazards can be avoided, and the less likelihood that students will want to have sex.

THE HARD FACTS

1. Sex is desired and enjoyed only by men.
2. Sex is not fun. Sex is painful, especially for the female.
3. Sex is hard work. Much like early factory production, sex involves hours of sweaty, tedious and mechanical labor.
4. To sum up, the man has all the fun, the woman only the worry: most importantly, of pregnancy and, less frequently, of death.

SIX SURE SIGNS OF SEX: THE EARLY WARNING SIGNALS

'But wait!" you exclaim nervously, and ask in an embarrassed mumble, "How do I know if I'm having sex activity?" The early warning signs of sex are easy to spot, and before your condition degenerates any further you may wish to take precautionary measures. Early detection of sex will prevent the unnecessary complications which arise from repeated sex usage, such as drowsiness, exhaustion, inability to solve quadratic equations and mental illness.

To assist you in your pursuit of sex care and prevention, we offer a brief checklist of symptoms. If any of these signals appear, **you could be having sex**:
1. Loss or peeling of clothing.
2. Sudden lack of interest in major sporting events, your senior thesis, stock market quotations, girls who "don't," mom and dad, and Eurocommunism.
3. Ringing of bells, singing of birds, sensing of the earth's axial rotation.
4. Guilt.
5. Disgust.
6. Sudden loss of respect for your partner.

THE MORAL QUESTION

At this point, we feel impelled to remind students that, unless engaged in by married couples for the purposes of procreation, sex is immoral.

BIRTH CONTROL

Having discovered that premarital sex is unpleasant and unethical, no further warnings should be necessary, at least not to anyone intelligent enough to read and write. Some of you, however, will feel compelled, either by "peer pressure" or by brute physical force, to have sex. In this case, contraceptive devices are your next concern in what is clearly a long series of reasonable objections to having sex.

To begin with, birth control is purely the woman's problem. As you probably know, men cannot get pregnant; women can. Face the facts, honey: when the doctor tells you you'll be eating for two and what's-his-name suddenly transfers to a foreign university, you're going to suffer, not he. Men do not like their women pregnant unless they're married. Remember: a pregnant woman is a fat woman.

So, ladies, here are your choices, none of them pleasant, and none of them safe:

1. **The Pill:** This pharmaceutical wonder, seemingly as harmless as a Chocks, will, after prolonged usage, make your uterus the laughingstock of your internal bodily organs. The pill causes your ovaries to unleash lethal electromagnetic waves which will turn you into a walking stockpile of radioactivity. After years of pill popping, you will have to be stored underground for fear of fallout.

1.

On the mildly but unconvincingly positive side, the pill is small, easy to take and readily available. Do not be fooled: cough drops have the same advantages and none of the unpleasant side effects, as well as coming in a wide variety of flavors. Pop a Vicks and tell your boyfriend you're too sick to have sex.

2. **The I.U.D:** An I.U.D. is a large, cumbersome device which is placed, or more accurately loaded, by a hydraulic air hammer in the woman's "sex place." The I.U.D., which is exceptionally ugly, scares potential babies away by making faces and rude gestures at them. Needless to say, it is exceedingly painful and, once inserted, refuses to leave its warm hiding place until the spring.

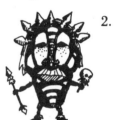
2.

3. **The Diagram**: The diagram is an explanatory flow chart which outlines the almost inevitable path from premarital sex to death. After sex comes the unwanted pregnancy, the forced marriage of incompatibles, the unfulfilling and nonremunerative job, alcoholism, suicide and disgrace. Once revealed by the woman to the man, the diagram will hopefully show the man the folly of his desires and he will leave well enough alone. If he persists, the diagram can be turned sideways and used to scar the male forever.

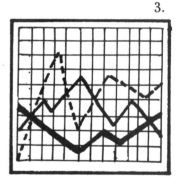
3.

4. **The Rhythm Method**: Make me laugh.

HOMOSEXUALITY

After a few years of sordid, uncomfortable relationships with members of the opposite sex, it will be only natural for you to consider redirecting your affections toward members of your own sex. If you found yourself nodding your head in agreement with this last statement, consult a family doctor or psychiatrist immediately.

CONCLUSION

The sexual revolution is over, and you lost. People of all age groups, particularly insecure college students, are now free to engage in interminable discussions of sexual behavior in a mature, guilt-free manner, while inwardly feeling more and more depressed about both the quality and the quantity of their sexual encounters.

College Confessions

September 1978

Volume 87

Number 9

75¢

My New Roommate's Luggage Was in Her Purse: She Came to Major in Men!

A New Cultural Center Wasn't All That These Afro Majors Were After!

My Varsity Boyfriend Was a Three-Letter Man: S-E-X

I Made a Mistake on a Computer Card and Had to Take My Classes in Mexico!

Department of Admissions: The Only Role the College Theatre Gave Me Was One in the Hay!

Special Exposé: Students Who Get A's — in Sin!

Dating College Athletes: All They Want Is a Quick Payoff Under the Table!

I Flunked Out of College by Reading Tawdry Gossip Magazines Instead of Paying Attention to My Studies!

My Alumni Society Wants More Than My Money!

METAMORPHOSIS OF A
COLLEGE ROOM

His freshman room

His sophomore room

Her freshman room

Her sophomore room

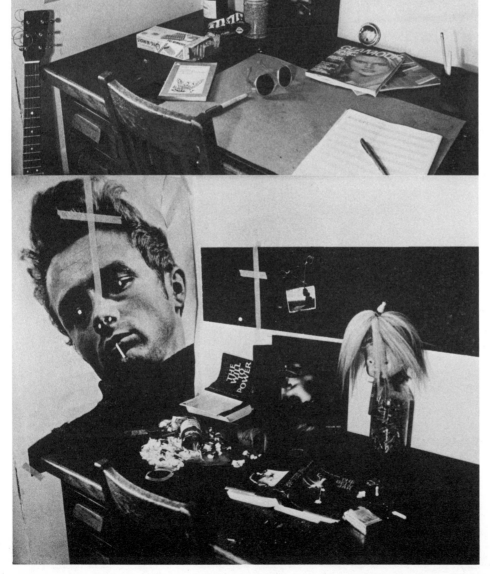

His junior room

His senior room

Her junior room

Her senior room

THE MEMORABLE
TALENT SHOW

The show's tonight and I just don't know *what* to do," fretted Madge Murdoch as she applied green gobs of slippery Dippety-Do to her flouncy auburn ringlets. *Drat!* thought the pert senior, *this hair seems to have a mind of its own today!* She had been drowsing all afternoon over her Civic Service textbook, and now it was too late even to make a funny costume for the school talent show. *If only I had talent, I'd show them — show them all!* But before Madge could continue, a familiar voice called her out of her reverie.

"C'mon, slow poke! Get a paddle and skedaddle! The show's gonna start in a few hours and the House Clean-up Committee wants us at Beagle Gymnasium pronto!" It was Pee Wee Wilson, Madge's best friend at Midville College.

"Pipe down, Pee Wee, I won't be but a minute!" responded Madge, Pee Wee's best friend at Midville College. Bounding over to her secret diary drawer, she scribbled, "Dear Diary, By the time you read this I will have gone to the big Talent Show, so wish me luck and wish me love, wmsh me this from God above. Sorry so short. Must fly! —Madge." And with that, the spunky cheerleader snatched up her ex-boyfriend's letter sweater and scooted out the door.

Dashing down the carpeted steps of her sorority house, Madge paused at the first landing to primp her bobbed locks and pull up her bobby socks, popping her lipsticked lips at the mirror as she did so. With a swish and a whirl of her favorite plaid shirt, away the ungainly tomgirl went, slithering down the banister in the plucky, devil-may-care fashion to which her pledge sisters had grown accustomed. Outside the house, Madge found Pee Wee speaking animatedly with a scruffy boy who answered to the name of Skeets Brody.

"Oh yeah?" sneered Skeets. "More wars have been fought in the name of Jesus than in the name of humanity, am I right or wrong? Answer me that, why don't you!"

"Well that's cuz humanity doesn't *have* a name, and Jesus *did*, so big schmiel on you!" spat Pee Wee, flustered by the persnickety boy's constant carping and sniping.

Observing the argument from her perch on the doorstep, Madge wisely held her peace until she felt it proper to interrupt. "Okay, you two tomcats, let's call it a day, whattayasay?" she said, her merry eyes bouncing between the two. "I mean, this isn't the U.N.!"

"Yeah, what's it to you anyway, ya big creepola! Now get outta my way. Scram, willya!" Skeets got up and rudely shoved Madge to the ground. "I'm going to be at the talent show tonight, and if I don't win, watch out, Midville College!"

Madge blushed for her friend Pee Wee. The two got along famously together, and were a well-known pair of "real troopers" around the campus. But Madge sometimes couldn't help thinking that her friend associated with, well, riffraff. Nothing good would come of this, she was sure of it. "I think you should seek professional help, Skeets Brody, you sure could use it!"

Just then Reverend Wrigley strolled by the little group. He had spoken with Skeets only last month, trying to help him with his "problem." No one liked Skeets very much after he had given Pee Wee's pet monkey a hot penny during their organ grinder show. "Even Toppy the monkey has more friends than you do" blurted Madge. "Isn't that right, Reverend Wrigley?"

The reverend spun on his heels and turned with a smile, a wave and a big hello. He never tired of such antics. His sprightly manner perked up glum spirits wherever he went. Raising one eyebrow slyly, he chuckled and said, "I'm afraid the girls have you over a barrel, Skeets — a barrel of monkeys, I'd wager."

The two girls fell into a fit of tittering over this bit of josh on the reverend's part and practically hurt themselves slapping their knees and hiccupping at Skeets' expense. But Skeets was unwilling to try things to their conclusion and took his leave by saying, "Just you wait, Madge Murdoch. You think you're President of the World or something. I'll fix you *but good*. I'm no fraidy cat — I'll murdelize you!"

Reverend Wrigley's eyebrows shot up. He knew Madge and Pee Wee to be fine young women, having attended many a community sing with them. "Now, hold on there, Skeets, you'd better take that back."

"The heck I will."

Instantly the strapping young paster collared the collegiate naysayer and toted him into the rectory. "You're coming with me, young man. You need a good talking to. Sore losers never show a lick of sense, Lord knows, but you take the cake!"

After they had disappeared into the chapel, Madge turned to her friend. "In all my born days I've never seen such a terror as Skeets Brody."

"Oh, those types are always the same, Madge. It's just that element that says, 'gimme, gimme, gimme.' That's all you hear from them. Never a nice word or nod. What a bunch of Marcus Mefirsts."

"My dad says he doesn't know what they're fighting for, but he figures they don't either," Madge squealed indignantly, showing the same vim and vigor that had won her an honorable mention at the State Pep Contest that semester. With such a boisterous personality, it was no wonder Madge was the heartthrob of the Campus Bobs. "We sure are a lot nicer than Skeets!"

"And how!" exclaimed Pee Wee. And with that, the two pals scampered off to the Campus Grill, where two well-deserved chocolate shakes awaited them.

As the two girls gulped down their delicious shakes, they mulled over their plans to decorate the gym. "I just wish we had some help from our fellow students," complained Madge.

"Don't get angry, Madge, get going!" said Pee Wee. "We have only just time enough to give the place a festive air."

"I — I — I'm sorry, Pee Wee, it's just that . . . what with the preparations for the show and all . . . I didn't have time to think of anything to do for it. You know, in the way of talent. And now that Skeets is angry at us . . . oh, everything seems to have gone wrong, all wrong!" The anxious campus leader broke into quiet sobs.

Pee Wee hooked her arm around Madge like a good school chum. "There, there, we all know you're a talentless hack. We don't expect anything more from you than we'd expect from a bath mat. Listen, I've sent Toppy to get your parents and bring them here so they can see the show. There, now are you happy?"

"Thanks, pal. I guess I shouldn't complain when there are so many people less fortunate than myself. You have it even worse, having an untalented friend like me!"

"That's right, Madge."

And so the two began filling salad bowls with M&M's and tying festive streamers to the gymnasium fans. Many hands make light work, and tonight was no exception. By the time curtain time call came around, so had half the students of Midville College, and work was finished in no time. Door after door opened and shut across campus as eager thespians converged on Beagle Gymnasium.

Madge peeked out from behind the curtains. Her parents had yet to arrive. As a Traffic Supervisor for the Midville Police, her dad was a pretty busy individual. Perhaps the shadow of crime was being pushed back a little further by her dad at this very moment! But the show would have to start without them. The audience was abuzz with excitement — what new talent would they discover tonight? But unknown to all, the show's fate was sealed.

Much to everyone's chagrin, Skeets Brody swaggered on stage first, even though he'd been scheduled to appear last. *There's just no stopping this ambitious ne'er-do-well*, clucked Madge to herself.

Skeets began by demonstrating how he had trained his plants to grow toward the sun. "Why, that's the same project he entered in the Westinghouse Modern Living Fair!" Pee Wee whispered. "That's that — Skeets is disqualified!"

Upon hearing the news, Skeets became disgruntled. "Okay, okay! *Now* I'm honked off!" he shouted, and off he stomped in quite a dither.

The members of the audience exchanged rueful glances and knowing wmnks. Skeets had done it again. He had cast an ugly pall over everyone's fun. But the resourceful girls knew what to do. Grabbing two coffee mugs from a backstage table, Pee Wee and Madge skipped onto the stage and began doing a vaudeville barbershop duet so that the audience wouldn't become restless. As the two eager-to-please pals cheerily hooted into their mugs, who should walk in but Madge's parents!

"Oh, Mom, Dad, I wasn't I didn't, I mean . . . I thought you weren't coming, and then I thought maybe something had happened, but it didn't, I mean you did, I mean you came after all!" Madge had to choke back the tears. "I guess I owe you an apology . . ."

But before Madge and Pee Wee could utter so much as a peep, Skeets Brody clambered up onto the stage — and with him was Toppy the monkey!

"Don't you come near me," Skeets ordered. "You've all had your fun with me, sure, but now I'm going to make sport of you — in more ways than one!" Running backstage for a moment, he returned with an oversized circus cannon, and a clown's mask. "Ha ha!" he chortled. "I'm always the clown, am I? So I'm a laugh and a half, am I? Well try laughing now!"

"He's gwine to fire de monkey at us!" shouted a befuddled Negro from the audience. And indeed the Negro's words proved prophetic, for Skeets quickly stuffed Toppy down the mouth of the cannon and struck a match on the barrel.

"*Now* who's over a *barrel of monkeys*, eh?" Skeets' eerie laughter echoed through the gym as he trained the monkey-laden cannon on the audience. At such close range, there was no telling how much damage the mammalian missile might wreak. The terrified audience cringed in tense anticipation, each onlooker praying that he or she would not be the victim of the crazed chimp-wielding gunman.

"Looks like Toppy's having a rum go of it," said Mr. Murdoch under his breath.

"Well, this is a fine pink tea I've made of things," whispered Madge to Pee Wee.

Then tragedy struck. Touching the lit match to the cannon's fuse, Skeets unwittingly set into motion the events which would seal his doom. Training the ape artillery on Mrs. Murdoch, Skeets breathed, "And now you must pay for your daughter's discourtesy, Mrs. Murdoch . . . ." A frightened gasp rose from the audience as one. Mrs. Murdoch found herself staring into the darling but deadly eyes of Toppy the monkey.

Thinking quickly, Madge screeched, "Skeets, look over here!" And with that, she "hung a moon" at him. Her marmoreal flanks glistened in the dim stage lighting as she waved them like a dancing bee. Startled, Skeets was taken in by the sly ruse of the resourceful senior. Madge's quick thinking had saved the day, for as Skeets turned to gape at her, he threw off his aim just enough so that when the cannon went off it sent Toppy sailing harmlessly through the open gym window. What happened next surprised everyone but Toppy. Once in the air the flying mammal reverted to his jungle habits and, spying the Midville goalposts as he careened toward them, reached out his tiny paws just in time. Swinging on the goalposts like a practiced gymnast, the scrappy chimp did a loop-de-loop which sent him sailing back through the window into the gym. The astounded audience looked on as a blur of monkey whizzed back over their heads and landed smack in the middle of Skeets Brody's chest. And when the smoke cleared, Skeets was dead, a monkey through his heart.

Miraculously, Toppy survived the incident unscathed. The happy pet clambered up his mistress' legs and cheeped triumphantly. "Eeeeek-eek!" said Toppy, his red and gold epaulets bobbing frivolously as he hopped and clapped his tiny paws. "Eeek-eek!"

"Now I've seen everything!" gasped Officer Clancy as he pushed back his cap to scratch his head.

"Well, if that don't beat all . . . ." mumbled a cranky old custodian.

But Pee Wee Wilson just shook her head, wagged her finger and smiled knowingly. "Well, Toppy, aren't you the bee's knees!

"We, the pledge sisters of Alpha Delta Pi," said Jocelyn Jiggers, "in appreciation of your abilities, award you, Madge Murdoch, this expensive medal because you have proven that you possess the ability to love others. And isn't that the greatest talent of all?"

Madge's mom and dad looked on from backstage, beaming proudly. As Madge received her medal, Mr. and Mrs. Murdoch were proud to have such a daughter. Madge tried to focus on the audience as the applause rose to a fever pitch, but her tears made it all look like a dream, a very, very good dream.

The next day Madge awoke and guessed she was just about the gladdest gal in Midville. All of the town's breakfast dailies carried photos of her "heroic act." The *Midville Missive* even put a headline over them, blaring, EM-BARE-ASSING STUNT BY COED SAVES TALENTED MONKEY. Madge put the paper down and allowed a smile to play over her lips. She knew she would cherish this memory for a long time to come, for it would be a long time indeed before there could be another memorable talent show.

CONSUMER REPORTS
LIBERAL EDUCATION INSTITUTIONS

Liberal education institutions are designed to cultivate a mind capable of clear, open and critical thought and to foster perfection of the soul. To test just how well they do these things we had our test crew attend three luxury liberal arts colleges (Duke, Harvard and Swarthmore), one economy-minded state education package (UCLA) and one anachronistic church-affiliated institution (Notre Dame). All testers began as faceless high school students contemplating law as an avenue to politics. After four years at college, all five were judged to have become better, more magnanimous human beings in some vague and undefinable sense. Institutions were, however, found to vary widely in their specific strengths and weaknesses, and sometimes in surprising ways. For example, Harvard, despite its higher tuition, failed to instill as profound an appreciation for the internal sympathy underlying all knowledge as its lower-priced competitors. Similarly, Duke scored disappointingly low in its treatment of metaphysical questions, while Swarthmore's "life-long habit of inquiry" was found to wear out after only five or six years.

THE FOLLOWING COLLEGES WERE JUDGED APPROXIMATELY EQUAL IN OVERALL QUALITY (LISTED IN ORDER OF INCREASING PRICE).

UNIVERSITY OF CALIFORNIA AT LOS ANGELES

Advantages: Affords California residents a surprising degree of moral perfection at a penny-pinching price; provides a well-rounded background in each of the major areas of intellectual inquiry — Natural Science, Social Science and the Media; particularly strong in uniting humanity in deeds with studied casualness in dress.
Disadvantages: Graduates, although willing to accept their roles as citizens of a free society, tended to prefer Monaco.
Prerequisites: Must be in the process of making a film decrying commercialism in college sports. A BEST BUY.

NOTRE DAME UNIVERSITY

Advantages: Attractive "super-Catholic" package offers an education with both profane and sacred components — secular knowledge for this world and spiritual training for the next; the only college claiming benefits beyond the grave — a good stretch-the-dollar investment. (Nevertheless, actual transcendent ecstasy due to mystical union with the imminent, loving God was rare, and such occurrences were usually over in a moment, albeit an eternal one.) Attractive campus; sailing in season; women shave their legs.
Disadvantages: Ideals of social service and individual self-development were never successfully united in a higher synthesis; social milieu favors brutish ignorance and moral turpitude; may be uninviting for shorter students.
Prerequisites: Some interest in contact sports as an activity to sublimate impure impulses.

DUKE UNIVERSITY

Advantages: Good treatment of justice and wisdom; grain alcohol punches; excellent stereo systems; year-round halter tops.
Disadvantages: Some slighting of ontological questions and glaring absence of a viable theory of perception; moral dilemmas fostered by links to tobacco money; fraternity deaths; sorority suicides.
Prerequisites: Cut-off shorts, a tan and a convertible.

SWARTHMORE COLLEGE

Advantages: Very good to excellent appreciation of moral virtue; attractive, clean layout; decorously remote from urban blight; acoustic guitars in abundance; leotards in season; social concern.
Disadvantages: Justice and magnanimity somewhat neglected (after graduation, our tester was still reluctant about accepting his role in a free society); anorexia nervosa required of sophomore women; reading of modernist poetry.
Prerequisites: A bisexual sibling.

HARVARD COLLEGE

Advantages: Good promotion of healthy soul, eloquence of speech, refinement of taste; abundant tasteful sherry parties; cultivates an arch amusement with the rest of the world; by senior year, even if our test student didn't know the correct answers, at least he was asking the right professors.
Disadvantages: Must be on constant lookout for egos raging out of control; hostile street urchins exceed recommended EPA levels.
Prerequisites: Some acquaintance with pronunciation of and spelling of "Sartre," **"Gesellschaft"** and "Truffaut."

MOBIUS

Loeb Drama Center
Harvard University

APPLICATION FOR EXPERIMENTAL THEATRE, SPRING TERM 1977

(To be filled out by director)

TITLE OF PLAY: Mobius
DIRECTOR'S NAME AND PHONE: Jason Leeds, Jordan K, 547-0526
AUTHOR: Hugh Hamburg.

Have you inquired into royalties, permissions, etc. for the performance of this play? (check) Hugh is my roommate and he's as into it as I am

What other staff have you contacted in regards to working on this production? Some buddies of mine from Jordan K are hip to the project; also, I put an ad in the Crimson.

Can this play be produced under the budget ($250)? 10-4.

Please discuss your concept of this play, what you hope to achieve by directing it, and any other relevant information. (Use back of sheet if necessary) Mobius by my roommate Hugh (or H.T.) Hamburg, is a modernist or, rather, post-modernist version of Melville Melville's masterpiece "Moby Dick." I have heard a great deal about the techniques of the "modern" or "post-modern" theatre, and I would employ them to this play. My brother Mark is a costume designer off-Broadway in New York, NY and could help with the costumes.
As Stanislauski said, "An Actor prepares."
(Hugh) Jason

Office use only: ACCEPT Maybe we can get his brother to come up for a "Learning from Performers."

Prologue

(The stage is barren, empty, unhappy. Voices appear and with them, bodies.)

NARRATOR: Call me Hugh. Some time ago--if you care how long, you're already missing the point because time doesn't matter and there really isn't a true time anyway I mean, not in the real sense.

WHALE: Call me Leviathan. I swim for my supper. I am white. I mean nothing, I mean everything. Time has no meaning.

AHAB: I am bestail Man, being that I am the primitive manifestation of what is truly within all of us.

HUGH/ISHMAEL: What is life, anyway?

AHAB: It is life itself.

WHALE: It is nothingness.

HUGH/ISHMAEL: What is life, anyway?

AHAB: It is death itself.

WHALE: It is being.

AHAB: Have you ever really looked into the sunset? The fire

OPEN CASTING FOR

A Mid-May Loeb Ex Production of

MOBIUS

A revolutionary experience of Melville's "Moby Dick"

by Hugh Hamburg '78

March 24, 25, 26
7-10 p.m.
Loeb Practice Room C

Loeb Drama Center
Experimental Theatre
Harvard University

Audition Sheet-Mobius

Name _Taylor "Slappy" Swanson_   Height _6'0 and strapping!_
Address _Hurlbut 315 or Lamont_   Weight _165 (in the day)_
(I'm taking 6 courses) (in the day)
Phone _8-3399 OR 5-1739 (in the day)_ Eyes _Hazel_
Harvard? Class? _Freshman/I'm from Texas-glad to know you._
Why are you motivated to appear in this play?
I would be interested even if I wasn't pre-law. Getting into Law School should be an academic concern, and should not infringe on the artistic pleasures in which I would like to participate ANYWAY.
What part(s) are you interested in and why?
I would like, if there is one, the part of the lawyer. If there isn't this part due to artistic pressures in the script, I'll take anything with a lot of social interchange with other characters.
If you are not cast, is there any area of technical work you are interested in helping on?
Any legal aspects of the production would be putty in my hands. I really enjoy doing it -- for myself. Leave it to me.
Previous Experience (at Harvard or elsewhere):
No real "dramatic" experience, but I play the prosecuting attorney ("devil's advocate") in many courtroom simulations in my freshman seminar on Law and Its Many Worlds.

Conflicts:
I am very busy with Soc Sci 2 and Gov 30, and may be late for rehearsals on schooldays. But as for personal conflicts, NO WAY!, because I am friendly and eager and good at social interchange.

Loeb Drama Center
Experimental Theatre
Harvard University

Audition Sheet-Mobius

Name _Dan Hick_   Height _Tall_
Address _The Keystone State_   Weight _Over_
Phone _No thanks!!! (Too technological)_ Eyes _2_
Harvard? Class? _Clown_
Why are you motivated to appear in this play?
My parents think I should round out my experience at college by participating in extracurricular sports.
What part(s) are you interested in and why?
Back Field, Linebacker, end. Because I know alot of good plays.
If you are not cast, is there any area of technical work you are interested in helping on?
I can plug things in. I know some hand tools. I also have alot of gum-backed reinforcements | You could use.
You don't want to know!!

Conflicts: _Sometimes I can't decide whether to put the toothbrush in the bathroom-holder or in its plastic case. Also, how far should I stand from the mirror? The toothpaste-spray from my mouth leaves unsightly white dots all over it and I look like I have albino chicken pox!!!_

Loeb Drama Center
Experimental Theatre
Harvard University

Audition Sheet-Mobius

Name _God_   Height _flexible_
Address _The Heavens_   Weight _flexible_
Phone Just call My Name loudly   Eyes ROYGBIV
Harvard? Class? _Of course, from the beginning._
Why are you motivated to appear in this play?

Well, I'm sick of being hidden, silent, listening to everybody else. I'm getting old and I want to be seen before I lose my looks.

What part(s) are you interested in and why?

Captain Ahab; I'm tired of being Mr. Nice Guy

If you are not cast, is there any area of technical work you are interested in helping on?

Previous Experience (at Harvard or elsewhere):

— Appeared in pillar of fire over desert
— Played trumpets on Mount Sinai
— Do a lot of work in dreams

Conflicts: Not available Sunday or Saturday mornings and five times a day on Friday.

Sheet 1 (top left)

Loeb Drama Center
Experimental Theatre
Harvard University

Audition Sheet-Mobius

You didn't have to underline this. I bet you didn't for Mr. Big Deal Bowling Pin Head in front of me. Like I have to read it well nobody can keep me from running right out of here. Try if die is what you want!

Name **Fuller Rehab**   Height **6'3 50/100**

Address **WJH 1066**   Weight **102**

Phone **They "took" it, See? They ≥ It!**   Eyes **Front**

Harvard? Class? **Right down this street. You can take my class but I get to keep the family Colorforms so Dr. Vincent gets real mad like he'll donk or bamp you.**

Why are you motivated to appear in this play? **Oh, I get it - a special question. Just for "help". Is what they say. Well, God won't let me "appear" any more because mother called the even number of times. I already said this.**

What part(s) are you interested in and why? **The water molecule, because it is small and can hide easy but can go anywhere like right into a whale's eyeball. Its lines are short and easy to say so your tongue doesn't fall back too far down near your heartbeat like it ALWAYS does.**

If you are not cast, is there any area of technical work you are interested in helping on? **If you have any loud talk-mouths I can fix them. Cause they like to trick (or hurt) you by saying they didn't mean it I always say. Then I laugh.**

Previous Experience(at Harvard or elsewhere): **Some experience at dodge ball but you use golf balls cause they least expect it. Also kicking orderlies (but they aren't) until they bend over and I can jab the needle into their brains through the ear cause they need it most if anyone does they asked for it.**

Conflicts: **This paper feels funny. Like if you stepped on a stick of chemical butter and you face lands in a nest of copper pine cones. What do you mean its an audition sheet a sheet is for sleeping or wrapping or climbing a sand dollar would know this.**

Sheet 2 (top right)

Loeb Drama Center
Experimental Theatre
Harvard University

Audition Sheet-Mobius

Name **Darryl Drayton**   Height **6'1"**

Address **Adams B-31**   Weight **140**

Phone **8-2121**   Eyes **Clearest Blue**

Harvard? Class? **Harvard '78**

Why are you motivated to appear in this play? **I so, so want to be in this play, I simply must tell you. I really, really must be in it, I'll just die if I'm not. It's a super, super, super piece of drama, and I'd love to dig my gorgeous teeth into it.**

What part(s) are you interested in and why? **Give me my little heart set on ... that doll of a sailor boy. When Ahab pulls that simply butch act of his, with that stuck-out stump, I'd really feel for my part, looking forward also to watching that old boorish whale spout and spew. I think its suggestive.**

If you are not cast, is there any area of technical work you are interested in helping on? **Not on your life, mister. I'd rather be caught red-glanded than be running around with those declassé "techies" of yours with their sweaty beards and gauche overalls.**

Previous Experience(at Harvard or elsewhere): **I've been around, buster, I played Prince Hal in a drag version of "Henry IV, Part 2", Prince Edward in a drag version of "Richard III", Hamlet, Prince of Denmark in a drag version of you-know-what, and art Prince in a drag version of "the Prince of Venice".**

Conflicts: **Emotional. Though I'm not violent by nature.**

Sheet 3 (bottom left)

Loeb Drama Center
Experimental Theatre
Harvard University

Audition Sheet-Mobius

Name **ANTOINETTE STOCK**   Height _____

Address **BERTRAM D-36**   Weight _____

Phone **8-6965**   Eyes _____

RADCLIFFE ~~Harvard~~ Class? **'78**

WHAT IS THIS? A PLAY OR A MEAT RACK?!

Why are you motivated to appear in this play? **BECAUSE I AM A WOMAN. BECAUSE I AM WOMAN. THE SEXIST THEATRE HAS OPPRESSED US TOO LONG!!**

What part(s) are you interested in and why? **THE WHALE. WHO SAYS THE WHALE IS MALE? YOU JUST ASSUME THAT IN THE SAME WAY YOU ASSUME WE ENJOY HOUSEWORK OR PUTTING YOUR SMELLY THINGS INTO — I COULD GO ON.**

If you are not cast, is there any area of technical work you are interested in helping on? **WOMEN'S STUDIES, OR SCRIPTWRITER WITH EDITORIAL CONTROL OVER SEXIST REMARKS IN SCRIPT**

Previous Experience(at Harvard or elsewhere): **PLAYED "FETUS" IN WOMEN'S HEALTH COLLABORATIVE ANNUAL SHOW.**

Conflicts: **MARCH 14,15,16,17**
APRIL 11,12,13,14
MAY 8,9,10,11

Sheet 4 (bottom right)

Rehearsal notes: 4-18

Scene 4

Ann + God: not enough tension; try more hate

Dan-stop looking up down Ann's shirt - it makes her nervous.

God - less vengeful, more loving with people; you can't play God with other people's lives.

* Call Felipe for slides of Attica for multi-media interlude. Music: Dead? Barry Manilow?

- Talk to Hugh about lengthening script, four hours seems too short

→ Modernism vs Post-modernism

Scene 21

Dan- hand-buzzer routine with whale does not work. Try something else - black soap? squirting flower?! (symbolic)

God - Not as mighty as you seem

* - Do Throw's rehearsal in nude, make sure Ann doesn't get paranoid

Premiere Society Offers Three Plays

by Margot Lane

When the Harvard Premiere Society takes over Loeb Drama Center, the stage becomes a mecca for avant-garde theatrics. I say avant-garde because the plays, written by talented students who are actively interested in art as a serious form of expression, are part of what I call the "new" dramatic experience. This "New" Movement (sometimes I capitalize it) is trying to break away from the traditional, or "old" type of classic drama epitomized by one of the true giants of playwriting, Shakespeare. These plays are opening up a whole new experience by examining the human condition and what's going on in general. They usually have a limited number of characters, and are even doing away with plot and setting as the average theatre-goer knows them. Occasionally strange things occur that the audience knows cannot really happen but they're alright because it's a metaphor. This progressive theatre is becoming popular in England, with playwrights like Tom Stoppard and Harold Pinter (the subject of a term paper) writing plays that have more than meets the eye.

The Premiere Society unleashed its first program of the season on an unsuspecting public last weekend, and your drama critic was on hand. The three short plays presented were indeed offbeat, but had a lot of inner meaning. The audience did not respond very responsively, but the fact that everyone didn't understand the plays as well as I did was probably responsible for the lack of response. Most of the Loebies were just out for a good time, drank a lot of beer and loudly explained to their girlfriends how well they would have handled a particularly tender rodeo scene had they not had soccer practice and made it to the audition on time. This is not the right approach to appreciating the Premiere Society. I was able to enjoy the show because I consider myself sensitive to new ideas concerning the never-ending mystery of living and beingness.

The first play, *Untitled #4*, proved to be a scathingly brilliant psychological thriller. It was written by Phil Foster '79, an "artsy" guy who happens to be one of my roommates, and adapted from two 1938 radio plays by Eugene O'Neill and Fred Allen, respectfully. The play expresses man's inhumanity to man through the central character Phillip. This is a clever derivative of Phil (Foster), so the play can be taken to be largely autobiographical in nature. Phil is supposed to be Lung Foon, a Japanese of Oriental persuasion. His parents come from Hiroshima, but because of radiation from the

From *Mobius* by Hugh Hamburg '78

Atomic Bomb he was born and raised Caucasian. His assimilation into American culture causes the kind of alienation many sophisticated people seem to enjoy. Since life is already serious, Phil decides to make it painful as well. Instead of spinning a web of intrigue, he inhabits a shabby 1-room apartment in the seamy part of the garment district. It is here where he lives his life of utter desolation, talking to no one, eating little, reading and sleeping most of the time. The room is also where the entire play takes place, and although it may not sound very entertaining in the sense that *My Fair Lady* is entertaining, it is entertaining in the sense that it makes you think. In Foster's world, thinking does not have to be a chore or a bore; it can be a thoughtful and moving experience. The lonely life proves as unbearable for Phil as for the audience, but he persists in order to be an anti-hero. Finally he turns on the television and later expires, drooling. I was sitting way in the back and couldn't see the drool, but Phil had told me about it in the room when he wrote it. I went to interview the star after the show to find out what he feels about this all-too-human character into whose shoes he steps each night at eight, but he had already left for a cast party.

During intermission I got up to go to the bathroom because I had to make. I opened the door but saw that it was too crowded, and I was afraid I would have to hold it in until the end of the show. I went out into the lobby and enjoyed a soda and some small-talk. When I went back to the bathroom it was empty except for a small, aged drunk who was at the last urinal, next to the window. He was wheezing and hacking like he had TB. I managed to keep from looking at him, but I thought about this a lot. I almost cried.

The final play was a real change of pace: a funny play. Entitled *Catskills*, it was truly a hilarious masterpiece of comic humor. Trapped inside a holiday resort during a summer thundershower, seven elderly patrons complain about the hotel's rude busboys, inadequate social director, and "generally lousy" service while watching the rain outside from a mah-jong table set up "special for them" on a sheltered veranda, just as the medieval Japanese priest watches the monsoon from the ruined temple in Kurosawa's brilliant *Rashomon*. For these men there will be no golf this August afternoon; for these women no Simon Sez by the poolside. However, their loss is our gain, since during the course of what might have been their agonizing afternoon (and play, essentially), we watch the hotel nightclub's off-hours comedians give their collective all to amuse and sedate the nagging geezers. I don't want to give any of the jokes away, but let's just say these cut-ups turn the place on its ear. At one point the chubby entertainer (probably a Buddy Hackett parody) does an imitation of Ray Charles by putting on a pair of dark glasses and yelling "I can't see a thing! Where the hell's the piano?" But I'm giving away too much.

By the way, there is an interesting production next door at the Experimental Theatre which I wasn't even supposed to review, but the other guy went home early for vacation. It is called *Mobius*, and I take it to be a modern reworking of Melville's *Moby Dick*, which I had to read for English 70. After having read most of the book and all of the Monarch's Notes, I considered myself something of an expert on *Moby Dick*'s plot, theme, and Review Questions and Answers. This new production has *Mobius* "stripped" down to its bare essentials, with only three characters performing the whole story. Frankly, I didn't think much of it, but I really don't see how it can miss, judging from the recent success of *Jaws*. Let's face it, a couple of guys and a big fish spell box-office bonanza in cold cash money terms. My regret is that owing to stage limitations, a real whale is not used — only a man trying to look like one and not doing a very convincing job of it. Granted it is a challenging role, but how is the audience supposed to empathize with the whale if he doesn't even look like one? And it's not at all scary. Would *Jaws* have scared you if the shark had been a small man with a mask trying to kill the fishermen metaphorically with dull philosophy? Of course not. *Mobius* could at least use some mechanical device, or a bigger man.

"I WONDER WHAT THE KIDS ARE DOING UP AT STATE...."

"I read an interesting article in *Us* Magazine at the beauty parlor today, dear," said mother. "It was about the 'new mood on campus.'"

"I read a similar item in the Wall Street Journal," said father, lighting his pipe. "By the way, honey; your hair looks *real nice*."

"Thanks for the compliment, sweetheart. But what about our children's hair? *Us* Magazine says that male college students' hair is moving down over the collar as fast as female college students' hemlines are moving up over the knee."

"The *Wall Street Journal* says that a major Eastern university has cancelled its annual Bible swim. And you don't need an accountant to tell you that *that* is bad for business."

"I don't know what to make of it. But, I wish President Jimmy Carter would look into the matter. His family is attractive."

"Can't agree with you there, loverbuns. The Federal Government already has its finger in too many pies. This is a problem for elected officials with *local* constituencies. Our nation is a republic, not a democracy."

"You know best, dear. But I can't help wondering what the children are doing up at State."

THE UNFORTUNATE COINCIDENCE

Sal pulls his last pizzas out of the oven at 12:55 a.m. One pepperoni, one mushroom, both large. By 1:03 Sal has locked up, and by 1:10 the pizzas have been safely transported to Baxter. Baxter is the most modern dormitory at the college, and it won some kind of award for innovative design with cement after it was completed in 1970. Paul says that this kind of architecture is popular in France, but Russ says that it looks like his grandparents' synagogue in a prosperous Florida suburb. The modern elevator is still broken, so by the time the four of us get the pizzas up the four flights to Baxter 405, the pizzas are cooling off. Hal is the one of us who's not Paul or Russ or me, and he will say something soon.

We were coming to the end of the midpizza silence that follows the prepizza chatter that accompanies walking the pies back from Sal's. The midpizza silence accompanies furious face-stuffing and is progressing to the postpizza chatter via the ceremonial argument between Hal and Russ over the last pepperoni slice and the last mushroom slice. Hal refuses to eat the mushroom slice.

"You know why. Later on when I belch, I belch up the smell of mushrooms and it makes me vomit."

"So why can't you eat the mushrooms and then have a Coke or an apple or something?"

"I could, but the mushroom smell would be in there enough to make me sick."

"But you already had mushroom!"

"I know, but why make it worse?"

Just then the door swings open and Ray Schweitzer struts in looking almost as pissed off as the time his roommate left a message that Ray's mother had died. That time Ray become incredibly upset, crying, throwing furniture, everything. His roommate got scared and told Ray that the message was just a joke; he didn't think Ray would react so badly. Ray didn't think the joke was funny at all and started spitting on his roommate's pillow. The roommate had the last laugh, though, when Ray found out that his mom really *was* dead. His roommate had only been kidding about the kidding.

Ray lives upstairs in 505, comes down all the time and talks a lot. When he sits down and begins his story, his anger becomes less alarming, more self-mocking and finally appealing.

"You're not gonna believe this. I can't believe it. You know what happened tonight? How could you know — let me tell you. I should kill him. He ruined it. He ruined my chance of sleeping with the most incredible girl I've ever seen live or on television."

We become interested as the last slice of pizza disappears (mushroom — into Hal, who would regret it later on). Ray continues.

"Let me tell the whole story. All right. There's this girl, Ilyse, who transferred here at the beginning of the semester from a state school back home. I went to high school with her, junior high, nursery, the whole thing, right? This girl is the most unlikely of combos — not only ridiculously, screamingly beautiful, but Jewish. And such a Jewess! She puts the "ew" back in Jewish.

"Okay, so it's rare enough to find a beautiful girl who has the blood qualifications for me to marry her. But this girl is further from my own particular brand of culture than an Indian. In fact, she looks like some Hindu goddess; this is no simple Queen Esther contest winner, but as ravishing as a Jewish girl can be without being Irish. For years I worshipped the girl, or parts of her, from distant

The Harvard Lampoon
Big Book of College Life

corners of the classroom. Gazing, you would think she was Mexican or maybe Italian. But as soon as she spoke, the jig was up. Not that she sounded Jewish, accent-wise. It was *what* she said. A *Rolling Stone* editorial walking the streets. Even worse, a poetess. Wrote everything in verse, no capital letters. And circles instead of dots. A circle over 'i,' a circle at the end of the sentence.

"Nobody could talk to her. Barefoot to school. Danskin bodysuits. As if a piece of Joan Baez had fallen off fifteen years ago and was still running around. Her father's a big attorney in town. So she hangs around being rich, smart, ravishing, and Jewish, only she does it with truck drivers and mechanics, who naturally are most capable of appreciating her poetry, her dissatisfaction with her parents' material values and that tortuous stretch of mountain road that travels down from her neck and disappears between her legs.

"She had run away from home and was living with some car salesman, or so the rumor went. Funny how everything Gentile has to do with cars. Anyway, she refused her parents' money after graduation and took some courses at the local college and fucked this guy and his cars.

"I hadn't really thought about her for a long time, and then all of a sudden I find out she's been going to college *here* since a few weeks ago when the spring semester started. I still can't believe I called her up. She barely knew me in high school, but sort of respected me because I'm such a genius I could talk on her level when I had the patience. But what do I care if she thinks she's too good for me? Let her sit through Godard films all day in a lotus position eating yogurt between mantras.

"I figured she probably doesn't know anyone here yet, so I'll call her. At worst she'll hang up, and at best I get laid, right? It might do me some good to get a Jew for a change, you know? Cheer up the folks. The shiksas are murder, bad for my nerves. Last one ruined my life. Irish, thin, beautiful, fragile. Got her away from some coal miner, some relative. All Gentiles practice incest. She thought I was some novelty act and slept with me for months. An idiot until I turned her on to the classics. The stuff Jewish dreams are made of: Kafka, Dostoevsky. She eats it up. All of a sudden she cools off, even though the sex gets wilder. Next thing I know she throws me out of bed one morning and tells me she never wants to see me again, but I should call once in a while to say hello and absolve her of guilt. Turns out she had read everything by Philip Roth over the past few weeks and discovered what an asshole either I was or she was, probably the former. She reads a book and she knows what we *really* think of them. After all this, I'm almost ready to try a Jewess only so I won't have to worry about her reading books.

"So two days ago I call Ilyse. Surprise, she's friendly, sure she remembers me, she knew I went here but didn't have the address and this and that and this and that. Plays the real intellectual. Starts talking about a film course she's taking. So Joe Stud asks her if she wants to go to a movie the next night and she says okay. I feel great.

"So we go to see *Blow-up* as part of the "The 60s: Cinema in Turmoil" festival. I thought it was a fine choice — intellectual, and everybody's seen it and knows what to say about it. So what does this idiot say? That she liked it, but she likes Hitchcock's other films better.

"We go back to my room. Between her Kerouac analysis and her tight T-shirt, I'm going out of my mind. She looks through my records. *Abbey Road*, she tells me, was 'the Beatles' first attempt at heavy orchestration, and then came *Help!* and the others.' She's saying that the theme from *Jaws* comes before Gregorian chant! She snickers at my *64 Original Motown Hits*. She says she loves jazz. She used to like George Benson, but lately he's really been selling out. This suburban snotface is telling me about selling out. She doesn't like the fact that Benson is on AM radio. Asshole! But I'm calm. Oooh, I'm good and polite and I agree with her. Do I tell her that I hate people who hate AM radio? No. Do I tell her that Benson starved for eighty years and if he wants to make some money he can do whatever he wants? No. Do I tell her that any superslick greased-up konked-out Negro wearing leopard skin leisure suits would be a zillion times cooler, funnier and more original than she is even if he went on the Carson show, joined the Doc Severinson band and married the Gabor sisters? Do I tell her that all I want is to be as black as licorice just so I can laugh in her luscious little rosy face? I should have called Benson to come over and rape her.

"So she loves jazz. Like, how cool is she? Does she want to hear *Kind of Blue*? She's never heard of it. The most famous, most coolascious jazz record ever she doesn't know from Helen Reddy. But I'm good. I put it on. She likes it. So we're groovin' on some Miles; it's cool."

Ray slipped into his hippest black voice.

"And because I'm cool, we're talking for hours. High school nostalgia. Anything. I vaguely remember the names Salinger and Carole King coming out of her mouth seriously in one sentence.

"Anyway, even though we're talking all night, it seems clear she doesn't want me to touch her. She just wants to sit and see if I follow her allusions. She doesn't realize that I'm the genius, not her. By this time I've got some Schubert on, and have given up hope. Then she tells me this amazing story."

If Ray had not said something amazing soon he would have been tossed out of the room. He continued.

"She got into a really strange mood. Maybe because I was the first face from home she'd seen in a long time. I don't know what prompted it, but all of a sudden she decides to tell be about the time she ran away from home. I think this is hilarious, and she made me promise not to tell anyone. The thing is, as she was telling the story she acted as if she were reciting some shopping list.

"She was seventeen, hated her parents and decided to run away and live with her boynriend in some trailer camp or something. Running away meant walking the two miles to where the guy lived. So she packed a bag one day and started walking, since her mother was out shopping with the car. She said all of this seriously. As she's walking down the street a small truck pulls up and slows down right next to her. There were three kids in the truck: some little fat guy, a big black guy and Joe DeLuca. Joe DeLuca was the biggest, toughest hood in the school and the town. Got three girls pregnant. Once beat up a teacher, then went to visit him in the hospital and beat him up again. Anyway, the truck just followed her step by step as she kept on walking. She was scared, but ignored the truck since she had to get on with her running away from home. The three guys started shouting obscenities and then pulled out fast. She was relieved, figuring kids like that always taunt a girl walking alone.

"She came to a pretty deserted area of town. Just then the truck pulled up out of nowhere and stopped right next to her. She kept on walking, a little faster, suitcase in hand since she was running away from home. The Negro was gone; DeLuca and the fat guy were the only ones in the truck now, and Ilyse was the only one on the street. DeLuca jumped out of the truck and ran up to her. She kept going; he walked alongside. He started asking her questions: where was she going, did she want a lift. She tried to ignore this. He put his hand on one of her breasts. She yanked herself away. He pulled a large knife. She froze, clutching the suitcase. He started feeling her up, right there in the road with nobody else around. He told her if she didn't get in his truck immediately he would stab her. In a state of terror she knew what he was going to do. Thinking as quickly as she could, she offered to go down on him as some kind of compromise."

Hal erupted. "Wait a minute wait a minute wait a minute. Ray, are you telling me that she told you all this? She actually said she offered to give the guy a blow job? She said it like that? In those words?"

"She told the story as coolly as I'm telling it now," Ray continued. "Her exact words were something like 'the safest and easiest thing to do' would be to suck the guy off. She said to him, 'Look, why don't you just let me go down on you?' She felt safer, and thought he would be less likely to kill her. She left her suitcase on the ground. He took her inside the truck. The fat guy was just sitting there with his hand to his mouth, giggling. DeLuca sat at the wheel, and she sucked him off while he held the knife at his side. The fat guy sat there watching the whole thing, laughing his head off. DeLuca, in the middle of all this, turns to the fat guy and asks, "Do you want a piece of this?" Ilyse, horrified and choking, was further repulsed at this prospect. But instead of answering, the fat guy just cracked up. Ilyse said her most vivid and terrifying memory of this ordeal was the sight of this guy rolling on the seat in convulsing hysterics. He laughed so hard that the laughter bypassed his vocal cords, and all she heard was the air screeching up from his lungs and pouring out of his mouth. She said she had nightmares for months from this awful laugh and that she would never forget it. Soon DeLuca came, threw her out of the truck and took off. She sat on the ground gagging and vomiting.

"She got up, dusted herself off and started running away from home again. The car comes back, this time with the black guy. She's so hysterical by this time that he doesn't even have to pull a knife. She gets right in the car, and he starts feeling her up even though she's puking her guts out. The guy panics as well as gets grossed out, and drives her to her boyfriend's trailer. Can you believe it? Her vomiting turns a rapist into a cabbie. She goes in and her boyfriend calms her down and then she probably blows him all night. End of story.

"Can you believe it? Whether it was true or made up, I knew she's nuts. What kind of girl tells a stranger this kind of story? I figured she was trying to tell me one of two things. Either she's insane and wants me to fuck her, or else because of the traumatic experience the thought of sex makes her sick. After that story, sex would have made *me* sick. She just sat there, staring into space, looking like she would fall apart any second. I judged her vacuous disinterest as an invitation to put my hand on her shoulder. Next thing I know we're all over each other. It's two or three in the morning already. She says she won't fuck because she likes to spend a whole night, you know, and she has a really early class in the morning. The next day, however, she can sleep late, so she suggests going out to dinner and then picking up where we left off. I acted as cool as the Coltrane which was playing over and over on the turntable. This is *Last Night*, remember. I told her I'd see her the next night, which was tonight, that she's beautiful and that the story about Joe DeLuca was a secret with me. She said she was glad finally to have a special friend here at school and snuck out into the night.

" Okay. Wake up this morning, ready to fuck all night. Run into Manny, whom I haven't seen in a few days."

Manny is an old pal of Ray's from high school who goes to college here also and a good friend to everyone in the room. Sort of a seventies college version of Lou Costello: people have a choice of laughing with him or at him and usually wind up doing both.

"Manny just got back from covering some concert for the college paper and wanted to tell me some stories. I figured they could wait, but I remembered that Manny used to think Ilyse was really cute in high school although he was too retarded ever to meet her. I doubted she had any idea who he was, so I thought I would introduce them and really impress Manny with my voluptuous acquisition. I told Manny I had a girl from home that I wanted him to meet, and that he should join us at South of the Border — you know, the Mexican restaurant — that night at eight. Tonight. I refused to tell him who it was.

"So Ilyse and I get to the restaurant first and sit down. I told her a friend from high school would be joining us. When I mentioned Manny's name, she said she had never heard of the guy. It really figured — why should Ilyse, a Bore to the

Core, have been interested in a truly hilarious human being like Manny? We had started in on the usual assortment of burritos and tostadas, when Manny strolled into the restaurant. When he came over to the table and saw who I was sitting with his eyes lit up and then he gave me a troubled kind of look. I figured he was happily surprised to see her but pissed off because I was the one who would fuck her. Hopefully Manny would try to pick her up anyway. You know Manny — he's a riot when he behaves as if he's capable of attracting anything female.

"When Ilyse turned around to see who it was, she dropped her enchilada. I thought that Manny, looking like a slob as usual, scared her a little. I had forgotten that the sight of Manny was enough to make any girl wince. Then she turned back and started giving me this really angry stare. I introduced the two of them and Manny sat down.

"Now, the two of them were both acting very strangely. Manny, whom you usually can't shut up, was just sitting there politely and grinning like an idiot. My guess was that he wanted to impress Ilyse and was trying not to act insane. Ilyse was being even quieter. She kept staring down at her plate. When she did look up it was to stare at me — she looked like she wanted to have a more intimate dinner, just the two of us.

"I was carrying most of the conversation. You know, usual stuff: professors, courses. I got to talking nostalgia about high school. Manny started giggling. To me it seemed like he was simply nervous about meeting this gorgeous babe, but then it got out of hand. He started giggling louder and louder and couldn't really cover it up. I started laughing too — you know how catchy something like that is. You guys know Manny; he cracks up at anything. But I couldn't quite figure out what I had said that was so funny. Ilyse kept giving me that stare. If I was offending her, I didn't know how.

"I thought that maybe the two of them felt awkward meeting for the first time like this after growing up in the same town. I told them it was strange they had never met before. Ilyse was shaking and started to cry. I got really upset. When I asked her if I had said anything to offend her, she just stared at me and kept crying.

"All of a sudden Ilyse jumped up and flew out of the restaurant. Naturally, I had no idea what the hell was wrong. I looked at Manny, who was in uncontrollable hysterics, and started laughing too. People around were looking at us. I gave up. I just assumed that Ilyse was still as screwy as ever. If the sight of Manny laughing makes her cry and run away — so let her. She's nuts, right?

"So I was sitting there shaking my head, when it all suddenly dawned on me. I couldn't believe it. I still can't. Watching Manny laugh, I realized that no sound was coming out of his mouth. Have any of you ever noticed that? When Manny cracks up, he doesn't make any laughing sound—just air coming out in spurts.

"I thought no, it couldn't be. Impossible. Manny doesn't even know the guy. I stopped laughing and asked Manny what was so goddam funny. And of course, he said exactly what I hoped he wouldn't say.

"That was all I had to hear, but Manny told me the whole story anyway. How could I ever convince her of a coincidence like this? Bad enough that the poor girl had to sit eating Mexican food with her assistant rapist. But she must think that I knew about Manny all the time, and that I intentionally asked him to come over and drive her to suicide. I'll never convince her I didn't know. I'll never see her in this country again. And I come out of this looking like King Asshole.

"Do me a favor and turn on the radio. AM radio. Find me the most overproduced, tuneless, sellout-sounding song on the air, and turn it up real loud. There isn't any pizza left, is there?

SEPTEMBER HOROSCOPE

VIRGO (August 22 to September 22): Watch out for men who ask you if your zodiacal sign is an apt description or the furthest thing from the truth. Also be wary of a poor student who offers you an overdose of dangerous drugs.

LIBRA (September 23 to October 22): September is *your* month for adventures! You will have new courses, new professors, perhaps even new roommates.

SCORPIO (October 23 to November 21): If you have an exam this month, study more than you usually would and you will likely receive a higher grade. Toward the second week in November, do not ride in damaged cars driven at reckless speeds by intoxicated individuals.

SAGITTARIUS (November 22 to December 21): Enjoyable club and fraternity functions may come your way, if you are invited to them. Socializing may not help your grades, but you may meet people who will be important business contacts in later life.

CAPRICORN (December 22 to January 20): If you go to the college theater, you may see a terrible play badly acted. Do not leave in the middle of the first act if you have any friends in the cast. If you go to the cast party, beware of lanky foreigners whose sexual preferences may be different from your own.

AQUARIUS (January 21 to February 19): If you spend your whole allowance on fashionable new clothing, you may have to take a job in the cafeteria. If you take your girlfriend to the racetrack, do not let her spend your money by betting on the ones with the cute names.

PISCES (February 20 to March 20): Expect invitations to romance at the beginning of the week, but beware of disappointments if your more attractive roommate suddenly becomes free for Saturday night. If you make social arrangements for your "trouble days," your date may be grossed out.

ARIES (March 21 to April 19): Good news will come regarding law and medical school, especially for those with boards over 760. Other pre-professional types should think twice about manual labor or the exciting range of new career opportunities being offered by the Armed Forces.

TAURUS (April 20 to May 20): Throwing things at your professor on the 28th or 29th may result in your receiving a lower grade at the end of the semester. If you drink heavily on the night of the 6th, you may experience some discomfort on the morning of the 7th.

GEMINI (May 21 to June 21): Secret information about the first test will benefit you more if you don't share it with the girl down the hall you've been studying with, so keep it to yourself. Keep quiet about love affairs if you don't want people to know you're not having any.

MOON CHILDREN (June 22 to July 21): Invitations to a junior college mixer answer your weekend plans. Don't get trapped or embarrassed.

LEO (July 22 to August 21): Negative you-know-what tests at the Health Services will allow you to forget that creep you spent the summer with once and for all. Unless you are a person that other people seek out, you'd better try to make some friends or you may never have any.

THE HARDY HAR HAR

The student magazine of Hardy College
"If we can make you laugh, let us."
Hardy Har Har is the official humor magazine of Hardy College, Moribund, Pa.

Send all correspondence to: Student Activities Building
Room 405

STAFF: Editor in Chief: LEN SCHWARTZMAN
Associate Editor: STEVE PERSKY
Business Manager: ROB LIEBERMAN
Art Editor: AL LEVIN
CONTRIBUTORS: Glen Weis, Phil Marcus, Steve Weinstein, Josh Kaplan, Eric Brodsky, Ruth Perlman, Harold Shefner, Michael Kaufman, Jeff Epstein, Don Messenger, Jack Schoefeld, Naomi Steinberg
SPECIAL MYSTERY EDITORS: Piro Sagnew, Nichard Rixon

EDITORIAL

Hi, everybody. As you may or may not know, this is the first issue of **Hardy Har Har** in over two years. Proper funding was the original problem since none of the stores in Moribund wanted to advertise because they already advertise in the yearbook and they felt that was enough. This year the administration is financing the first issue and hopefully it will get us off the ground. Frankly, we hope it gets us on the ground — and out of the sewer! (Which is where we are now, beneath the ground.)

But seriously, lack of interest was also a problem. Not this year, baby. Just look at the masthead — we've got a large and diverse crew, all of whom have heard their fair share of zingers and creasers. We pity the poor Young Republicans Club, whose headquarters (if they have heads!) is right next door to our new office. They're going to get a whole lot of ribbing this year — plus lots and lots more. After Watergate we're afraid the Young Republicans might try to "break in" to our office while we're "breaking up" the university with our issues. With typical **Hardy Har** horseplay, I myself personally called up next door in my Gerald Ford voice, asking for Richard Nixon, and demanded the rest of my money for the pardon. They haven't called back yet to congratulate me on my little gag,

so if they can't "get" the joke by now, let them stew in it.

But what is really "our brand" of humor at the **Hardy Har Har?** Well, you won't be reading any jokes like the ones Bob Hope tells or Lou Costello either, although we respect these men for their achievements in comedy. We want to go a litte further for a more intellectual no-holes-barred approach. We will go past rib tickling and give readers a **Hardy Har** heart attack from hilarity.

What do we think is funny? Everything and everybody. That's right. We're not afraid of raising a few eyebrows around here. This place could use a few laughs. It's a college, and schoolwork and competition often create a tense and competitive atmosphere. We know this, and we'll try to loosen things up by "lampooning" everything under the sun. We feel we can fight pretension by making people laugh at the world around them and themselves. We're not ashamed to laugh at ourselves and you shouldn't be either. If students see the humor in school, they will have a better time, grow in wisdom, be more relaxed and, in the end, get better grades.

Hardy har har,
Len

LETTERS

Dear Sirs,

Your last issue really cracked me up.

> — *Humpty Dumpty*
> *Off the Wall*

Dear Sirs,

Your last issue was a pain in the ass.

> — *Maria Schneider*
> *Last Tango, Paris*

Dear Sirs,

I didn't get any of the jokes.

> — *A Pre-Med*
> *Hardy College*

(Editor's reply: It figures!)

APOLOGY

    In our last issue two years ago, we made some cracks about Professor Herman Tyler and what a hard marker he was. Last year Prof. Tyler was stricken with paralysis and asked to retire. In all fairness to the professor we must apologize and ask someone to hold this up for him to read. He never really marked that hard, and those who did not receive honor grades in his classes, when all was said and done, probably deserved what they got.

    We may have gone too far in our satire of Hardy professors, and we're the first to admit it when we pull a boner. We teased the man only out of respect.

PICTORIAL PIECE: A DAY AT THE HARDY HAR HAR

The Hardy Har Har office is a little different from most of the other places on campus — a kind way of saying it's really weird around here!

Our Editor, a serious man.

Working on issues is serious business. The magazine is always on our minds.

But we still take a serious interest in schoolwork.

Our writers work hard and seriously coming up with funny gag material. Well... maybe we're not as serious as we think!

A STRANGE DAY
by Glen Weis

Some days everything goes wrong, you know? Last Friday I had a big test in Biology. I studied all night and read all the notes. The joke was on me, though, because it turned out that test was really in Math! I don't know if I studied the wrong things or if they just asked me the wrong questions. Afterward I went home and got really shit-faced!

After the test and drinking, I was really hungry. So I went to the cafeteria. The thing is, they had the one food I don't like — egg salad! Also, the soda machine was broken!

When I got back to my room, my roommate's parents were there, so I couldn't even smoke a few joints. When they left, his girlfriend came. The thing is, she's really ugly, so I left the room. I started to finish a term paper, but it turned out it was missing. The thing is, it was stolen by a pre-med!

Later that night I went to the big dance. You know how ugly the girls were? The girls were so ugly I thought it was a cattle show! And the band sounded like they were playing classical music!

I went home to go to bed, but the thing was, my roommate and his friends came back from a beer blast booting all over. The sound and the smell of the barfing kept me up all night! I guess he wasn't sick or anything!

HARDY HAR HARTOONS

If a picture is worth a thousand words, then Hartoonist Al Levin has quite a mouthful to say as he takes a few playful potshots at... yup, you guessed it — our very own campus!

"Oh, you take the pills **before?**"

Hardy Girl: You conniving, money-hungry cheat!
Hardy Boy: I may be bad, but I'm not a pre-med!

"What is this stuff — steamed shit?

THE CASE OF THE MISSING NOTES
by Steve Persky

Private eye Sam Shovel, who was also a Hardy student, sat at his office desk, which was also his dorm room desk. His secretary, Miss Shapely, brought in the first client of the morning. It was another Hardy student, Joe Blow. Joe admired the secretary's legs as she stepped out of Shovel's room.

"Your secretary certainly is shapely," he commented.

"You bet she is," replied Sam Shovel, grinning because the joke was that her name actually **was** Shapely.

Joe continued. "Here is my case, Sam. I was in the Science Building doing an organic chemistry lab. I left a solution to settle with my open notes right next to it while I went downstairs to the Automated Soda Shoppe. When I came back, my solution had turned a green color, when the expected precipitate was yellow. I analyzed it and discovered that Kool-Aid had somehow gotten inside. I reached for my notes, and they were gone!"

Sam surveyed the situation. "I smell sabotage."

Joe gasped. "Surely you don't mean..."

"Yes," Sam agreed. "I suspect a pre-med in your class wants to see you drop a few grades. Doesn't anyone have anything against you?"

"Only the girls on campus!"

Sam exclaimed, "Can't you be serious for a minute?" although he himself could really appreciate Joe's gag.

"Well," said Joe. "There is a pre-med on my floor who's mad at me. He was a big Ford supporter and has Republican posters all over his room. Well, one day I broke in and put up Jimmy Carter bumper stickers, pictures of jackasses and posters of Adlai Stevenson. I even left peanut shells in his room."

"Blow me away!" cheered Sam. "No wonder he's mad at you. I'm sure he stole your notes for revenge. Let's go!"

Shovel and Blow went to the Reformatory Dormitory and knocked on the door of Room 405.

"Open up!" demanded Shovel. "We know you're in there, Gus Oontite. Give us those notes or we'll tell your parents about that C plus on the Biology test!"

Finally the two broke open the door. And what did they find. Gus Oontite was lying dead on the floor, his wrists slashed by a dissecting knife from Bio Lab.

"Looks like he got himself before we could. That C plus probably was too much humiliation," said Shovel. Blow searched the room. Then he said, "Bum me out. It doesn't look like my notes are here. All I can find are these stacks of *How to Prepare for SAT* books!"

Then the two left the apartment. Then Joe saw, on the street, a page of his notes. And then another.

"Look, Sam," said Joe. "My notes! They're falling out of that man's briefcase. Do you suppose he's our man?"

Then the two ran after the man and they finally saw who it was... none other than Richard Nixon!

"Tricky Dick," said Shovel, grabbing the suitcase. "The jig is up."

Nixon started yelling, "I am not a crook."

"Oh, yeah?" exclaimed Joe. "Then how do you account for the notes?"

"Well," admitted Nixon, "after my exit from politics, I decided to go into medicine. So I'm taking pre-med courses at Hardy."

Shovel asked, "Didn't your H_2O-gate experience teach you anything?

"Sure," said Nixon. "Peace with honor grades."

As punishment for his crime, Nixon was forced to take Professor Kapper's course*... for two whole semesters!

*Editor's note: This is kind of a private joke for students in Prof. Kapper's class. Prof Kapper is known by his students as being famous for giving lots of work, and also for being a Democrat.

Section

5

Paradise
Lost:
Graduation
And
The
Afterlife

BEVERAGES

COFFEE	SM	LG
COFFEE	30	50
TEA	25	45
ICED COFFEE OR TEA	45	70
MILK	35	70
FOUNTAIN SODA	35	60
APPLE CIDER	55	95
LEMONADE	35	60
JUICE	30	55
CANNED TONIC	35	
LIME RICKEY PLAIN OR RASPBERRY	45	85

it's the real thing Coke

SAND		SUB	SAND		SUB
95	B L T	1.45	1.35	PEPPER OR CHEESE STEAK	1.85
85	CHEESE BURGER	1.35	1.15	ROAST BEEF	175
1.25	CHICKEN SALAD	1.75	135	RB & SWISS	195
1.10	CORN BEEF	1.65	105	STEAK	165
70	EGG SALAD	95	110	TUNA	155
75	GRILLED CHEESE		105	TURKEY	145
75	HAMBURGER	1.20	110	WESTERN	135
1.05	HAM	1.55			
1.25	HAM & CHEESE	1.70		ALTERATIONS	
65	HOT DOG	1.10		CHEESE	.15
1.45	MUSHROOMBURGER	1.95		SWISS	.20
1.35	PASTRAMI	1.85		TOMATO	.15

DESSERTS

CAKE	45
DOUGHNUTS	20
DANISH	45
TURNOVERS	45
ICE CREAM DISH	55

OMLETS

CHEESE	149
HAM	175
HAM & CHEESE	195
MUSHROOM	185
MUSHROOM & CHEESE	255

Enjoy Coca-Cola

TEN REASONS NOT TO GET A JOB

1

You have to work.

2

It's habit-forming. Once you get a job, you'll want another, and then another. Many college graduates think, "Sure, I'll get a job. I might as well just try it and see what all the fuss is about. Everybody else is doing it. I can quit when I want." Well, they're wrong. They'll soon be caught in the vicious cycle of employment addiction. It's better not to start at all. Why do you think they call it work?

3

Once you stop being a student, you can never go back. Remember those pathetic people who came back to hang around your high school? You'll look even sillier showing up at mixers, pep rallies and Sadie Hawkins dances after you've taken a position in a respectable accounting firm.

4

It's unbearably tedious. Not only that, but employees and their families are not eligible to win.

5

You will have to carpool with a sullen adolescent typist or a Hindu engineer/mathematician who "loves speaking my new language of English."

6

Taking a job means taking on *new responsibilities*. Before you know it, you'll be married to an overweight hypochondriac with four sickly brats with crooked teeth and a house in the 'burbs. And those remote-control garage openers aren't getting any cheaper. You'll have to take out insurance policies on everything from health care to rodent invasions. Then you'll have to worry about your kids coming home with Puerto Ricans who spray-paint their names in Day-Glo colors all over your living room walls. Soon you'll be seriously considering buying a hairpiece and purchasing a condominium in Fort Lauderdale or the Rio Rancho Retirement Village. All this can be avoided by the simple decision not to take a job.

7

People will start calling you "Mister" or "Sir." Hippies will resent you and call you a "capitalist roader." People with better jobs will shake their heads and say, "What a waste of human talent." In minutes, you will lose the respect of everyone.

8

Fully employed people can never have sex.

9

You'll have to say nice things about the boss' new "flamethrower red" polyester golf pants, laugh at the boss' jokes about people who mismanage their personal finances and carry on endless conversations with your boss about "pennant rallies," "the primaries" and "resort areas." You'll have to nod your head with conviction when he refers to his employees as "a team" that works together to "bring home the bacon."

10

If you take a job, you'll be an adult.

MEXICAN MEDICAL SCHOOLS

A Message from the Chairman of the American Medical Association

In recent years, American medical schools have experienced a severe decline in applications. The reason? *Recruitment drives* attempting to lure our best students to *Mexico*, a land of deceit and treachery, of deadly bees and charging bulls. Anything goes in this land, where killing is a sport and Ricardo is a middle name. There is only one solution to this depletion of our precious pre-medical resources, and that solution lies in education. (Reprints of this bulletin available.)

. Travel agents do their best to make the country look like a scenic paradise. But look again. "Sand" is actually grated fiberglass, tough on American feet. This ocean is so polluted with tequila that recently thousands of sea animals beached themselves for a protest rally.

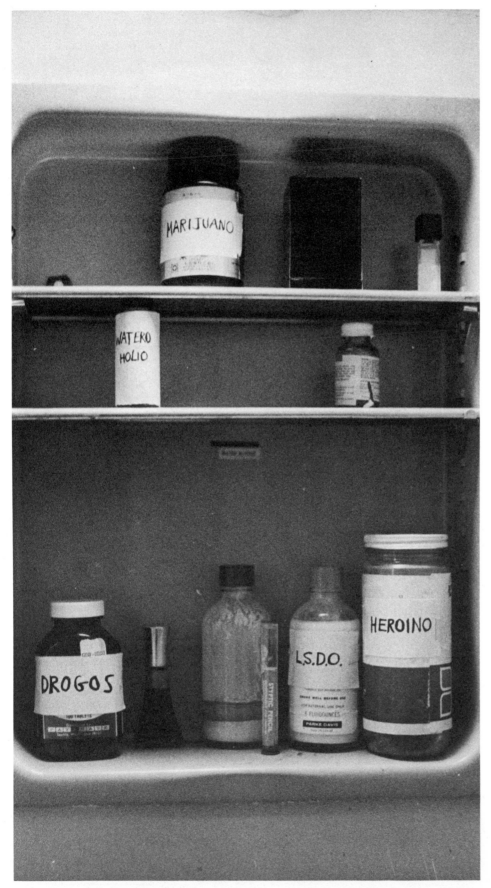

. Hospital facilities are woefully inadequate. This medicine cabinet must supply a 6,000-bed laetrile clinic.

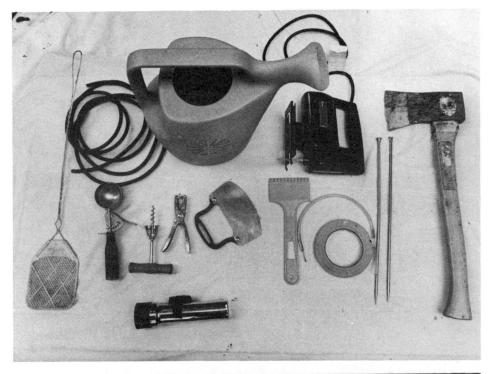

. A typical set of surgeon's instruments, Durango style. Close examination reveals that they are covered with insect pests. Not shown is the Mattel Vac-U-Form used for all plastic surgery.

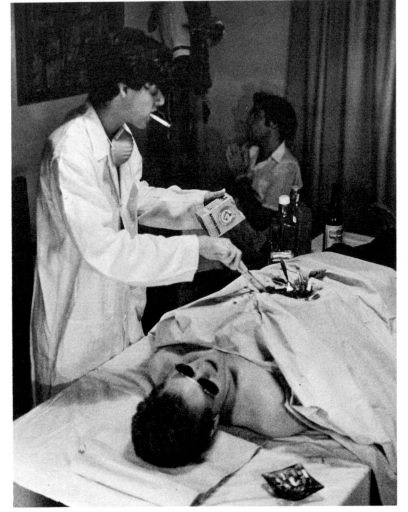

. In a common Mexican operation, the surgeon inserts a box of Arm & Hammer in the patient's stomach to absorb harmful food odors. Note gila monsters being used to clamp arteries — crude by American standards.

. "But don't doctors rake in the dough down there?" Here is the unvarnished truth. All transactions must be made with enormous Aztec calendar disks, the official coinage. Monstrous wallets like this one ruin the lines of most suits.

. Paper money? You'll need that for weekly incentivos (bribes). In exchange, your room will be protected from iguana attacks and late-night visits by mariachis (noisy tramps).

. The overabundance of Mexican M.D.s, who constitute 18 percent of the population, has made hospital or private practice impossible. Recent graduates must look for less conventional positions — i.e., torture supervisor in the local prison. Here, the doctor supervises as two sadistos (guards) administer a sedativo (brutal beating).

. The lucky few are able to find government jobs — perhaps inoculating souvenirs or explaining school bus accidents. Others less fortunate are forced to seek employment as lawn ornaments.

TAKING TIME OFF

In the anxiety-ridden, high-pressure atmosphere of college life in the back-biting, dog-eat-dog seventies, students have turned with increasing frequency to the expedient of "taking time off." This allows them to step back from the college scene and examine themselves, their college careers, their options for the future and the world outside educational institutions.

Let's be frank: these people are wimps and losers, the ones who complain about the meaninglessness of existence while those around them climb over their backs, get lucrative jobs and really hit it off with the opposite sex. These are the people whose "friends" would sell them down the river for a six-pack. These people are fools.

But what can we do with these social pariahs besides sticking out our tongues at them and saying, "What's the matter? Can't take it? Huh?" Let's take a look at a typical time-off-taker and compare him with a successful, well-adjusted student who has no inclination to leave his comfortable, balanced collegiate life which oh-so-effectively blends study, sport and socializing.

The time-off-taker (TOT) is characterized by his frazzled hair, his three-day growth of beard, his unwashed clothes and his tormented expression. He is revolting. His hometown girlfriend left him for a gas station attendant with a fast car and tattoos of mass murderers on his bulging chest. He is very concerned about the depletion of our fossil fuel reserves. His father thinks he's a creep, and for once Dad's right.

The well-adjusted student is healthy and happy. He is secure in all social environments. He studies hard, plays the game by the rules and wins every time. His dad is a wealthy industrialist who can get his son any job he wants. Okay, he's a slimy, butt-sucking moron, but in years to come, he'll be calling the shots.

Now let's look at what the TOT will be doing in his time away from the groves of academe. In order to explore themselves, students can choose one of three and only three alternatives to the high-powered way of life found on college campuses: traveling to exotic lands (i.e., Europe), staying at home doing nothing or taking a high-powered, impressive-sounding job.

Travel: With a backpack and a Eurail Pass in tow, the TOT heads off to **do** Europe. Once there, the TOT discovers that Europeans take their foreign language instruction much more seriously than he ever did, even to the extent of using these languages in their everyday activities. In fact, foreigners actually appear to be thinking in a foreign language. **What a bunch of show-offs**, the TOT will think, and scream at them the names of famous American baseball players.

After spending his time on the Continent, the TOT will have received valuable training in deciphering train schedules and in looking bewildered and pathetic, skills which he had already mastered by going to college. Upon his return to the campus he finds that everyone is bored by his travel anecdotes and groans at his pretention. The TOT resolves to go back to school, work hard and make a lot of money.

Doing Nothing at Home: At home, the TOT mourns the loss of his high school insouciance and plays a great deal of pinball. He tries to establish a new, more mature relationship with his parents, who, when alone, talk about what an amazing leech he is. After a few months of killing time, the TOT resolves to go back to school, work hard and make a heap of money.

The Fancy-Schmancy Job: The TOT sees an opportunity to leave behind the disadvantages of college life — a sheltered environment, interesting and well-informed peers and exciting intellectual pursuits. At the same time, he can retain

"Are you going abroad on a fellowship?"
"No, on a cattleship."

all of its advantages — tedious work, ass-kissing and back-stabbing — by getting an impressive job in the real world. Almost all of these jobs are in Washington, D.C., or in medical research laboratories, where the TOT evades the stifling routine of pre-professionalism through an association with para-professionals.

Once he begins his job, the TOT realizes that there are no mixers or frat parties outside college. He becomes increasingly aware of the fact that once out of school, all human beings become increasingly cretinous, make jokes about the weather and have lengthy discussions on the relative merits of athletic teams. The TOT decides to go back to school, work hard and make a big stack of sawbucks.

In case we have not made our point clear yet (THE POINT: TAKING TIME OFF IS FOR HOMOSEXUALS AND FAILURES! MAYBE IT'S FINE FOR THAT GREENBAUM BOY DOWN THE STREET' BUT NOT FOR OUR SON), let's take a look at some case studies from our files.

Barry T.: Barry T. was a "big man" at his Midwestern high school — captain of two sports teams, president of the student council and a straight-A student. He arrived at a highly prestigious Ivy League college with a career in journalism in mind but with a strong desire to learn anthropology. Barry was quickly knocked down to size. He did poorly in his classes, never got laid and was ridiculed for wearing cowboy outfits and displaying a lively interest in the commodities market. Put off by the insane, pre-professional grind, he chose to take time off. After a year of "bumming around the world," Barry was determined to go back to college, work hard and get into a good law school. Unfortunately, while in Europe, Barry contracted a rare strain of cholera and died.

Susan D.: Susan attended a swank private school in New York City where she finished at the top of her class, became incurably anemic and read a lot of plays in French. At college, she discovered that everyone else dropped phrases like "Ou est la salle de bain?" and "Je suis Guy de Maupassant" while drinking espresso and smoking Gitanes. Susan became unstable, mispronouncing German idioms, confusing the names of fashion designers with those of French existentialists, and setting off firecrackers in large lecture halls. It was time for her to get away, so she went back to Park Avenue and sat out a semester.

After developing and then dissipating a true passion for The Dance, attending the premiere of every avant-garde cultural event, having affairs with every professor in the NYU Philosophy Department, Susan resolved to go back to school, work hard and be accepted by a good law school.

On her way back to school her train derailed, ran into a truck carrying propane gas and exploded.

Vince I.: Vince was a poor boy who made good. He overcame his lowly socio-economic station and ethnic affiliation to earn a full four-year scholarship at a small liberal arts college on the West Coast. Vince's habits, among them armed robbery, extortion and assault with a deadly weapon, made him unpopular. The school consisted entirely of wealthy aesthetes who cut Vince dead figuratively until he returned the favor literally by murdering seven of them during a free-speech rally. Vince took time off at a federal penitentiary in Ino County. He made up his mind to go straight, apply to another school, work hard and be accepted by a good law school.

The day before he was to be released, however, Vince was taken hostage by other prisioners who demanded better meals and an exchange program with foreign criminals. The prison officials laughed heartily, and so, to prove their seriousness, the other inmates slashed Vince's throat with a broken light bulb.

As you can see, only misfits take time off. All of them end up with a fanatic desire to attend law school. All die before they can make their dreams come true. Stay at school. Better a live pre-alcoholic than a dead pre-professional.

ARE YOU OUR TYPE?

"This letter from Entwerp Enterprises is not centered on the page, and it contains many erasures. Cancel our million-dollar contract, Miss Hurt, and find me a supplier with a secretary who can type!"

"This phone message is handwritten! I'll never get any work done."

It isn't all work! *Two fun-loving members of the copy set dance the rollicking Tabular Shift at the student-run Spacing Bar, a favorite haunt of Happy Fingers uppercasemen.*

Professor Emeritus Everett M. Budd, holder of the world land speed-typing record, is able to type in a dozen languages and dialects. He's dead now, but his colleges live on and will be pleased to serve you!

AT THIS VERY MOMENT, SOMEWHERE IN THE WORLD OF HIGH FINANCE:

The powerful tycoons depicted above are not figments of our imaginations, nor are they alone in their desperate plight. Hundreds and thousands of valuable dollars are wasted every day by greedy secretaries and office assistants who never took the time to master the most basic commercial basic of all: careful typing. Even the very best handwriting in the world won't win back those squandered dollars! Typing, and typing alone, can make up the difference.

Don't backspace into a low-paying "job." Happy Fingers Institute of Typing graduates earn up to one hundred dollars a week with their abilities. We could be the magic margin of success in your clerical future. Clip the coupon below and visit our attractive campus.

"Now I earn a lot of money and make fewer typing errors!"
      —A happy graduate

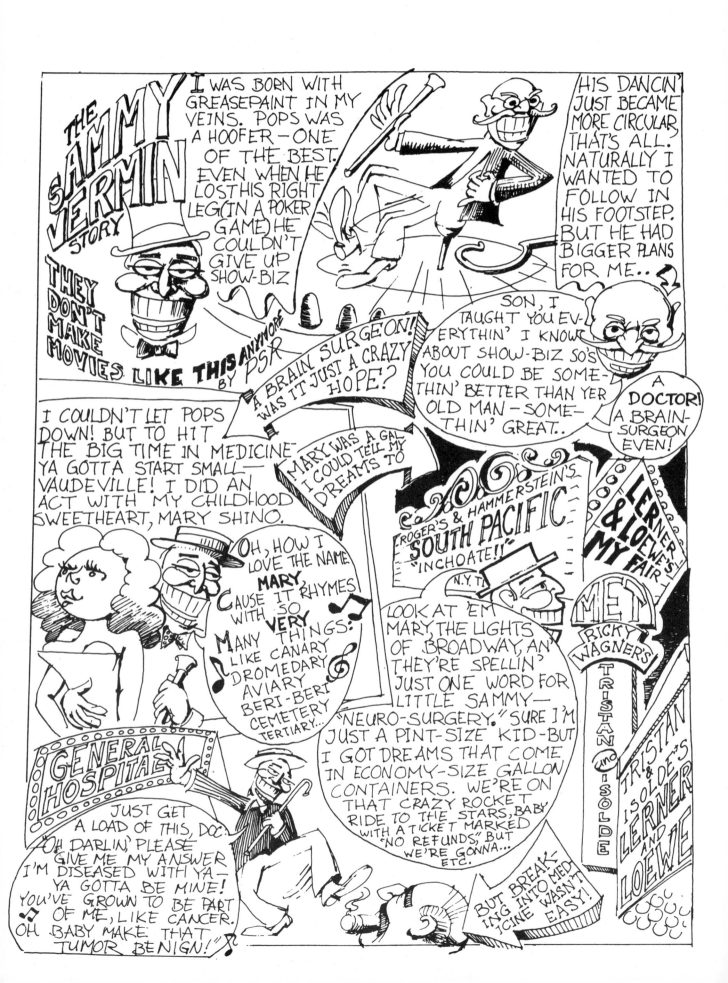

HARVARD UNIVERSITY
OFFICE OF CAREER SERVICES
& OFF-CAMPUS LEARNING

CAREER PAMPHLET NO. 81

OGCP

CASE STUDY NO. 59
"LOWERING YOUR SIGHTS"

Many Harvard undergraduates suffer from the illusion that the Harvard name will guarantee lucrative employment at graduation. This, sadly, is simply no longer the case.

Although some students each year are able—with a certain degree of luck—to secure a job shortly before or after commencement, we find that in general the student who has not found a job by the end of his junior year often faces the degrading prospect of unemployment. Therefore, unless an undergraduate's projected grades and board scores indicate a successful application to a major law or business school, he is urged to begin seeking gainful postgraduate employment as early in the sophomore year as is possible.

OGCP emphasizes the importance of keeping an eye out for likely opportunities while doing such everyday tasks as reading the newspapers (eg. the obituary section is often helpful in discovering recent openings) and also of developing "connections" which may prove useful and/or profitable in the years to come.

OGCP suggests that the student start optimistically and then lower his sights gradually until sinking to the level of his acceptability.

Case study Number 459 shows the employment effort of James W. Ackley, a typical member of the class of 1974.

PORCELLIAN CLUB

October 22, 1973

J. Willingham Ackley, Jr.
Eliot House O-22
Harvard University
Cambridge, Massachusetts 02138

Rearden, Taggart, Galt & Branden
642 Wall Street
New York, New York 10038

Dear Mr. Rearden:

I am currently a Senior at Harvard and will be graduating this spring with honors in economics. I am writing to express interest in a junior executive position with Rearden, Taggart.

To offer some background, my family is originally from Westchester, but we have since moved to Grosse Point Farms, Michigan. My father (Har. '44) worked for firms in these areas before retiring two years ago. Perhaps you have met my roommate's father, Marty Thurmond of Thurmondite Incorporated (makers of Thurmoplast Dentu-Cling), sometime on Wall Street.

I went to Hotchkiss before coming to Harvard where I have been quite active in the Young Republicans, the Ayn Rand Society and the Bull and Bear Club (I also ran the Eliot House Model Stock Exchange last year). I am currently the Harvard campus representative for Gillette's "The Dry Look" distribution and am a stockholder in Maharishi, Inc. After spending last summer as a messenger on the floor of the NYSE, I have dreamed of a career on the Street.

I subscribe to Fortune, The Wall Street Journal, Money and Forbes in order to keep up with the exciting changes in corporate finance.

I have found at Harvard that one must always be wary of the irrational and radicalized political atmosphere of the campus. I have sought to avoid this since I feel that most products of such influences are incompatible with the dynamism of today's corporations.

As noted above, I am majoring in economics with special concentration in the subject of East Asian natural resource development. I have dealt with case studies of numerous areas that are excellent prospects for mutually beneficial commerce.

I feel that this is an exciting time not only for development in emerging nations, but for continued growth in America. I would like to be a part of it.

Sincerely yours,
J. Willingham Ackley, Jr.

The Harvard Crimson
The University Daily — Founded 1873
14 Plympton Street
Cambridge, Massachusetts 02138
Tel. 547-2811

January 29, 1974

James A. Millman, Editor
Ramparts Magazine
287 Debbs Street
Berkeley, California 90431

Dear Mr. Millman:

I'm finishing off my Sr. year at Harvard and will be entering the real world this spring. I'm writing to let you know that I'd really like to become a staff writer for Ramparts - especially in the field of my major - radical economics.

Having lived on the fringes of decadent capitalism for 21 years - my father was a chauffeur for limo firms in Westchester and Grosse Point until he was crushed by the exploitative system - I believe I have seen enough to be of value in the fight against the bosses of wage slaves everywhere.

After going through the academic rat race here, I have found that what goes on in Ivy heads doesn't amount to a cow turd when compared to the truth and reality of the street. So I've spent my time as the Eastern Mass. coordinator for Common Cause, as a reporter for the school paper and as a correspondent for the Angela Davis newsletter.

I subscribe to The New Republic, The Berkeley Barb, Challenge and, of course, Ramparts in order to keep up with the movement.

I have found at Harvard that one must always be wary of getting sucked into the Establishment and dragged down into middle class apathy. The products of such selfish and apolitical thought are incompatible with today's prospects for revolutionary change. We must be ready.

As I said, I'm doing radical economics here with special concentration in the subject of capitalistic exploitation of Southeast Asia. I've come across a number of disgusting cases of virtual rape of natural resources by American corporations that should be excellent subjects for exposés.

I feel that this is an exciting time not only for raising the consciousness of a decadent society, but for the emergence of such ideals as yours. I would like to be a part of it.

Yours,
Jim Ackley

May 24, 1974

James W. Ackley
Eliot House 0-22
Harvard University
Cambridge, Massachusetts 02138

Mr. Martin Thurmond, President
Thurmondite Incorporated
Thurmoplast Dentu-Cling Division
Thurmondvale, New York 10082

Dear Mr. Thurmond:

Bill said to let you know that he is fine and was accepted at
the Law School.

Do you by any chance have any openings in your accounting
department?

Sincerely yours,

James W. Ackley
James W. Ackley

July 13, 1974

Jim Ackley
Cambridge YMCA
1134 Massachusetts Avenue
Cambridge, Massachusetts 02137

The New Jersey Turnpike Commission
Division of Toll Collection
13 W. Arnold Street
Hackensack, New Jersey

Dear Sirs:

I graduated from college this spring with a degree in economics.
I was also the Treasurer of two student groups and have friends
who will certify that I make change well.

Could you let me know if there is an opening for a toll booth
collector at anytime? If there is one, please call the
Cambridge YMCA at (617) 868-7593 and ask for Jim Ackley, the
one with all the books.

Thank you.

Sincerely yours,

Jim Ackley
Jim Ackley

August 14, 1974

Buddy's Grill
2481 Cambridge Street
Cambridge, MA

Buddy -

You still need a pit man? If not, I would be interested
in the dish washing job if that's still open.

Thanks alot.

Jim

HARVARD UNIVERSITY
CAMBRIDGE, MASSACHUSETTS

August 30, 1974

Jim Ackley
% Sanctuary
483 Mt. Auburn Street
Cambridge, MA 02138

Massachusetts Unemployment Compensation Office
14 A John F. Kennedy Bldg.
Government Center
Boston, MA 02114

Dear Sirs:

I have been unemployed for the
requisit 12 weeks & have not yet
received my first check.

Please remit check to me %
Sanctuary, Cambridge, MA 02138.
Thanks.

Jim Ackley

**Mr. Ackley has recently secured employment as a soda jerk at Brigham's
in Harvard Square and intends to contribute $20 yearly to his class
fund.**

CONNECTIONS

I'm your kinda guy. Put er there. Can do. You betcha. I got a million of em. I hear you. Don't I know it? Say, what's yer number? I'm there. Name yer poison. Can I give you a lift anywhere? Well, maybe just one for the road. Listen, I know where you can get one for a song. Can I get you a cool one? What was your name again? Didn't quite catch it. Nice, nice, real nice. I like it. I like it so much I even love it. Sign here. You scratch mine, I scratch yours. I mean, what are friends for? Any time I can help a friend. No bother — really! I mean that; I sincerely do. Look, can I help it if I take a liking to a smart young fella like you? Say when. When. Ha-ha-ha-ha. That's a knee slapper. Tell that to my boss! Don't let this get around, but he's not what he makes himself out to be. The big Buckola, you know? Sure, the Almighty Dollar. Drinks like a fish — looks like one too! Where have I heard **that** before? Tell that to my boss! So I says to him, I says, you can take your requisition slips, and you know what you can do with them! I said that. I did. We ought to get together sometime and talk turkey. Don't say that again or I might just take you up on it. Well, as long as **you** don't mind. No skin off my back. Trouble? No trouble at all. No, really, I'm serious. Tell that to my boss! Hey-hey, a friend in need, dot-dot-dot, you know? No offense, mind you, but I hear tell the whole department's on the skids. Take it from me. Have I ever steered you wrong? Look, you up shit creek? Here's your paddle. Plain and simple. Stick with me and you'll be getting a little something extra in that paycheck come Friday. You caught us with our pants down, frankly. All kidding aside, we could use a desk jockey with your kinda savvy. What kind of outfit are we running? Your kind of outfit! It'll work just like a dream. Ha-ha, a real sharpie, aren't you? Okay, five big ones. That's what I like to see, team spirit, a company man! You got it in you, I can just feel it. That's what **she** said. Ha-ha-ha-ha! Some kinda guy! Tell me, how long's it been? That long, really? Nooooo. Look, give me a buzz tomorrow. Meet you in the Wreck Lounge of the Beer 'n Beef. Where do we go from here? Everywhere, that's where.

APOLOGY FROM
DOUBLEDAY & CO. INC.

Something terrible has just been brought to our attention. An illegal and highly unethical method of psychological manipulation has been employed by the writers of this book—with you; the reader, an unsuspecting victim.

Perhaps you have heard of the marketing technique known as subliminal advertising. In the visual sublimation procedure, some message, usually in the form of a graphic image, is viewed by the subject for a split second. The subject is not at all aware that he has been exposed to any message at all; nothing is perceived by the conscious mind. It then can control the subject's decision-making process, making him do anything—even run around naked.

Until it was outlawed by Congressmen terrified of being seen with no clothes on, this strategy was used primarily in movie theaters and on televison. A brewing company flashes an image of a beautiful woman drinking beer during a daily soap opera; she is surrounded by handsome and adoring men. That week thousands of housewives add cases of beer to their shopping lists, neglect their children and become alcholics. A soft-drink company strategically substitutes a picture of a hot, arid desert for three frames of a film. The man in the theater, exposed to the image for a third of a second, feels a strange tingling in his throat and goes over to the refreshment stand, where he buys fifty one-pound bags of sand. (The strategy backfires if the man is an idiot.)

When we commissioned the Harvard *Lampoon* to write this book, we as publishers had no idea that the writers, really just a bunch of kids, had it in their power to extend this subliminal advertising to the medium of print. By working in collusion with our printers and the Harvard University Psychology Department, the *Lampoon* writers were able to send subliminal images through *the pages of this very book*.

For those with little scientific background, the process employs a chemical agent that responds to light reflected from the page at a certain angle. The effect is similar to that of those "moving postcards" parents used to buy for children at the World's Fair instead of sugary treats. Unfortunately, the *Lampoon* has used this scientific achievement selfishly to manipulate you . . . and you . . . and you.

For example, take page 112. It certainly looks harmless enough to the *naked eye*. But a special "advertisement" has been written in special chemical ink which goes unseen by the conscious eye but is drilled into the subconscious mind. It reads:

BUY A SUBSCRIPTION
TO THE HARVARD *LAMPOON*
SEND $5 TO 44 BOW STREET
CAMBRIDGE, MA 02138

and then continues with some nonsense about sending poverty-stricken children to football camp with the money.

This message can be consciously "seen" only by scientists wearing cobalt-irradiated glasses or by cataract patients who would have the book read aloud to them anyway.

Other subliminal advertisements for *Lampoon* subscriptions on different pages mention that the "Harvard *Lampoon* is the nation's oldest humor magazine as well as the funniest periodical in the world" and that "staff editors have included John Marquand, George Santayana, Robert Benchley, Fred Gwynne, George Plimpton, Donald DeFrieze, William Gaddis and John Updike."

One subliminal image on page 57 shows a man buying a *Lampoon* subscription and then driving a diamond-plated car while surrounded by beautiful women. Another subliminal image on page 97 shows a man not buying a *Lampoon* subscription and then attending the funeral of someone he loved very deeply. A falling safe is inches from his head.

This kind of advertising is cheap and unlawful, and we are sorry it had to happen. Because of the time and expense involved in the printing process, these advertisements could not be removed before this edition went to press. Fortunately, there was still time to insert this message. We hope that no readers will fall victim to this criminal marketing technique, and we urge everyone **not** to subscribe to the Harvard *Lampoon*, 44 Bow Street, Cambridge, MA 02138.

We repeat. Do **not** send $5 in check or money order to

The Harvard Lampoon
44 Bow Street
Cambridge, MA 02138

Sincerely,
Doubleday & Co., Inc.
Publishers

continued .

DOUBLEDAY
A COMMUNICATIONS CORPORATION

Message To Readers

Do not be fooled by the preceding message. It was not written by Doubleday, but by a <u>Lampoon</u> editor well versed in the science of <u>reverse psychology</u>. We are the real Doubleday & Company. Because of the time and expense involved in the printing process, the phoney letter could not be removed before this edition went to press. Fortunately, there was still time to insert this message.

By telling you NOT to suscribe to the Harvard <u>Lampoon</u> the editors think they can trick you into actually WANTING to suscribe - that is, psychologically speaking, to DESIRE a subscription in wish-fulfillment terms.

Since we do not want you to buy a suscription, we will counter this reverse psychology by urging you to buy a subscription to the Harvard <u>Lampoon</u>, 44 Bow Street, Cambridge, MA 02138. We repeat: definitely , by all means send $5 to

The Harvard Lampoon

44 Bow Street

Cambridge, MA 02138

We tell you this in the hope that you will not do so.

Sincerely,
Doubleday & Company Inc.
Publishers

Message to Readers !!

Looks like we got here just in time. The last message was written by a LAMPOON editor disguised as a proponent of reverse psychology, but he is actually well practiced in forward psychology. By telling you to buy a subscription to The Harvard Lampoon, he only wants you to do so. We are terribly sorry for this inconvenience.

Prices do have a way of going up. So, in case the person reading this is not you, but your grandchild, or child, or someone else's child, please be warned that the price may have gone up to $10.00 or even $5.25 or some other outrageous number, and don't be surprised if the lucky people who are manning the Lampoon offices when your letter arrives tell you just that.

The preceding book was written and drawn by the following members of the **Harvard** *Lampoon*

Kurt Andersen
Allan Arffa
Henry Beard
Lee Bearson
Andy Borowitz
Carter B. Burwell IV
Stephen Candib
Steven G. Crist
Christopher Dowd
James Downey
Stephen Fenichell
Bruce Ferguson
Sanford Frank
Ian Frazier
Thomas Gammill
John Gillespie
Ann Hodgman
Mel Horan

Douglas Hughes
George Johannessen
Bill Johnsen
Caroline Jones
Patricia Marx
Brian McCormick
George Meyer
Mark O'Donnell
Jackie Osherow
David Owen
Roger Parloff
Homer Pettey
Mitchell Pross
Paul Redford
George Rohr
Charles Stephen
Ted Trimble

and a small host of illustrators who never signed their work.